The Journe ... ne

Chris Thomas

The Journey Home

ISBN 186163 041 7

Cover photograph by Ella Baker
Cover design by Paul Mason

Published by:

Capall Bann Publishing
Freshfields
Chieveley
Berks
RG20 8TF

Dedication

To all those who question and to Diane who let me share her magic carpet.

Our deepest fear is not that we are inadequate.

Our deepest fear is that we are powerful beyond measure. It is our light, not our darkness, that most frightens us. We ask ourselves, "Who am I to be brilliant, gorgeous, talented, fabulous?

Actually, who are you not to be? You are a child of God. Your playing small doesn't serve the world. There's nothing enlightened about shrinking so that other people won't feel insecure around you. We are all meant to shine, as children do.

We were born to make manifest the glory of God that is within us. It's not just in some of us; it's in everyone. And as we let our own light shine, we unconsciously give other people permission to do the same. As we're liberated form our own fear, our presence automatically liberates others.

Nelson Mandela

Contents

Introduction

Planet Earth is unique. Of all the planets in all of the star systems throughout the universe there is no other like Earth. No other planet has so much free water on its surface. No other planet has such an oxygen rich, dense atmosphere. No other planet has such a multitude of diverse life forms. Most importantly of all - no other planet has a magnetic and physical density that is anywhere near to that of Earth and is capable of supporting life.

This uniqueness also applies to the human life forms that inhabit Earth. So why is it that Earth is so unique?

In recent years, there has arisen a new form of literature which purports to give answers to life in the form of channelled messages. All of these channelled writings have had their relevance and many, in fact, are of great importance to humankind at this time of transition.

However, none of these books have attempted to tackle our basic, fundamental longing for answers to the age old questions: who are we? Why are we here? Are we alone? What relationship does Earth and its multitude of life forms have to themselves and to the universe as a whole? The answers to many of these questions have been available since humankind appeared on the planet, but over the centuries, they have become hidden by personal interests and clouded by repetition and dogma.

As mankind undergoes a shift of consciousness so vast that all of the past centuries must be left behind, the underlying reasons for humankind's existence have to be re-discovered and put into their proper perspective.

This book does not pretend to have all of the answers, but is intended to bring these issues into a sharper focus and hopefully, light into some of the darker corners.

This book is also intended to promote thought and discussion on these issues so that we can all move forward together with a clearer understanding of ourselves and humankind's place in the greater universal community.

Chapter One

The Recent Past

The world is at an end! Armageddon is upon us! I think not. These are the headlines that so many people hear and see that it pervades the most exciting time in human history with an air of darkness and gloom instead of light and new hope.

The period at the end of 1996 and the beginning of 1997 saw the ending of the old life, as humanity has experienced it, and the dawn of a brighter, freer future. These are the most exciting events that have happened during the 7000 years of recent human history.

Gone are the dark days of karmic re-cycling and suffering relegated to a past that most are already starting to forget and what has begun is the birth of a new human existence so far removed from human experience that most have not recognised its coming. Four events took place between August 1996 and January 1997 that have altered our planet and ourselves forever.

The Heart Chakra

The planet has always functioned in much the same way as the human body. It is composed of and is maintained by the free flow of energy through its Chakras and Meridians.

The existing chakras and meridians, or ley lines, have served their purpose well during the whole period of human and planetary history between Atlantis and the present. However, to accommodate mankind's transition a new, more powerful, system is required.

The existing ley line and chakra system was put into place in the early days of the Atlantis period and was modified at the end of Atlantis to accommodate the sinking of that continent. The affects of the grid has varied over the intervening centuries as man's consciousness has ebbed and flowed to the dictates of world events and humanity's needs. The draw on this freely available energy has reduced as mankind's levels of consciousness reduced and minimised their interaction with the planetary consciousness. The seven global chakras provided energy frequencies that reflected the energy requirements of the physical body until such time that mankind was ready to change.

However, in order to reflect humanity's current change of consciousness, a new ley line grid and new chakra centres are required. The new chakras were put into place a little over 20,000 years ago when recent human history began. However, they were not activated at that time as human chakras were not able to accommodate the higher frequency levels. As our 20,000 year plan is nearing its completion and human consciousness is changing, a new energy is needed to help in the transition process.

Approximately 50 years ago a new ley line grid system was begun which overlaid and interacted with the existing ley line grid and connected to the soon to be activated chakras. This work was carried out by a small number of humans and what would currently be described as "Angel" helpers. The new grid is very carefully constructed to interact with the old grid to provide a new energy source for both the planetary consciousness and for people. The remaining two outcrops of Atlantis, Britain and Ireland, have always been at the forefront of human development and planetary consciousness. Given this history and connection, the new grid and heart chakra is centered on Britain. This is not jingoism nor any attempt at re-establishing Britain's global influence but a quietly stated fact of the history of human consciousness. The inhabitants of Great Britain are no more, and no less, than a part of humanity's whole and have chosen their land of residence as a higher consciousness decision to be a part of humanity's current change.

On August 14th 1996, in a remote valley in North Devon, the final connection to the new "Heart" chakra was made and the new ley line grid activated. A great deal of preparation work was carried out by a small group of people, over a long period of time in order that this connection could be made. Most of the people involved in this work were unaware of the final purpose of their efforts but all had an overwhelming sense that their work must be done and is a clear indication that each individual, whether working alone or collectively, can make a very real contribution and a very real difference.

The exact location of the chakra is unimportant but the energy contained within it is of a far greater strength of range of frequencies than has been available at any time during mankind's history. All people can draw upon this energy either for themselves or for their work with planetary cleansing.

For the technically interested, the frequency range is from 8Hz to 53,000,000,000,000 Hz and is truly a limitless source. The switching on of the "Heart" chakra, the term "Heart" is used in the sense that it is the primary energy source that "pumps" and feeds energy into the new grid and chakra system and does not correlate to the human heart chakra, had two effects at the time of activation:- firstly, the "switching on" of the new grid and the other twelve global chakras and the thirty nine lesser chakras, and secondly:- to emit a low frequency pulse of energy that re-activated some of the so-called "junk" DNA contained within human body cells. DNA is the primary human memory system and re-activating this section of the DNA brought about the beginning of mankind's final re-awakening.

The thirteen global chakras are located as listed below, they are not given in any particular order nor do they relate to human chakras but are major energy centres on the new global grid.

Devon	-	Great Britain
Constantine	-	Algeria.
Wan	-	Central African Republic
Calvairia	-	S. Africa
Kanpur	-	India
Perun	-	Russia
Ust-Nera	-	Russia
Tai Nan	-	China
Ketapang	-	Borneo
Quilpie	-	Australia
Kamloops	-	Canada
Leon	-	Mexico
Lake Titicata	-	Peru

Avalon

To many, the realms of Avalon have belonged in the "if only" category and forms a part of a distant memory that cannot quite be taken hold of. The realms of Avalon were removed to a place of safe keeping over 900 years ago as man's destiny changed and Christianity's influence began to overlay the ways of the land.

Avalon's influence was removed with extreme reluctance. Humanity was beginning to enter a new phase of experience and experimentation and if the energies and peoples of Avalon remained as part of the changing human consciousness their love and energy would have been abused and eventually destroyed. By taking Avalon out of human grasp and altering perceptions they could be saved until such time as man was once again ready to accept the lives of the "little people" as a safe reality. Human awareness and levels of consciousness have altered so dramatically over the last thirty years that it has been possible to consider bringing Avalon back into the physical dimensions.

The "little people" that remained within human spheres have always worked with the planetary consciousness maintaining our world as close to a physical paradise as human activities would allow. However, they have tended to hide themselves away as they have a deep seated and justifiable mistrust of human motives and human activities. Despite this mistrust they have continued their work with great love and humour and have taken great delight in interacting with people who have been aware of their presence.

Due to the work of a growing number of people of acceptance and working with the "little people", it was felt that it was possible to begin forging stronger links between people and the fairy folk. In order for these links to develop and strengthen, the influence and energies of Avalon needed to be re-connected directly with human physical dimensions.

On August 16th 1996 the first bridge between the two worlds was made. This bridge is not permanent. Trust needs to be re-developed before Avalon accepts its true role in planetary and human affairs. Never the less, the link has been forged and Avalon's influence is amongst us once more and the magic that is Avalon can once again enhance all of human activity.

It is now up to all of humanity to show Avalon that its trust is warranted before a permanent link can be established.

The Karmic Process

That which could be described as very recent human history, that is the last 7,000 years, has been lived in order to live out an eye for an eye re-cycling process that has commonly been called Karma. The act of re-cycling in this way was instigated in order to experience all that there is to experience whilst occupying a physical body.

The soul, or consciousness, has cloaked itself in flesh in order to become human and undertake these experiences as part of a much longer human cycle that has spanned 20,000 years. As the 20,000 year experience is coming to its end and human conscious awareness is beginning to expand to its original level of understanding, the need for karmic experience has diminished and finally came to a close with the ending of 1996.

At the start of the 20th century, humanity as a whole, began a process of clearing the 7,000 years of cause and effect. This has led to many conflicts arising on personal, community and country levels that has produced so much conflict and resolution during this century. We have seen the removal of apartheid, the undermining and destruction of closed and oppressive regimes and the opening up of global communication and access. They have all been a part of the final clearing that has needed to be undertaken in order for humanity to clear out its past. 1996 was the year in which the conflict came to an end. The light of reconciliation and understanding shone very brightly. Christmas 1996 saw the mending of family rifts and misunderstandings as all outstanding karma was settled. This is the new reality:- Karma no longer exists.

The New Consciousness

Most people are aware of another element of human consciousness - that which is commonly called the "Higher Self".

The term "higher self" should really be described as Higher Consciousness as it refers to a disassociated element of an individual's whole being. The Higher Consciousness is the greater part of the human soul that is the keeper of memories and is the director of an individual's life. Due to a number of reasons that are described in later chapters, human existence has been maintained and experienced by only a percentage part of an individual's total consciousness. The completion of the karmic process has allowed humanity the space and the freedom to begin the process of consciousness integration.

The new freedom has allowed for other clearances and other resolutions that relate specifically to this current lifetime, 1997 is the year that is to be used to finally resolve these situations. Whilst this clearance is continuing, the new energies that will allow full integration of the total consciousness are slowly being incorporated into each individual. The new energy began working with our system in January and was finally and firmly in place on April 27th. 1997 is the year in which humanity finally began to regain its unity.

Chapter Two

The Story Behind the Headlines

The first chapter briefly outlines some of the more important recent events in our history. However, to understand these events and to put them into context, we have to look at our origins. This book only deals with human existence and does not incorporate the other forms of life that exist throughout the universe except where they specifically relate to us. Our foremost connection is with a group of six civilisations that do not have a solid form as we understand it. This group of six, collectively, we would usually call the "Angels".

The major determining factor in our lives has been the planet itself. We exist on a planet that has energies and densities of energy that are peculiar to it. These energies are that which make us physical. The best example of density varying with energy is that of water. At its highest energy level it is steam, in its normal condition it is liquid and at the lowest end of its energy frequency it is ice. The physical and chemical composition of the water is the same in all three instances the only variable is the amount of energy contained within the atomic structure of each water molecule. On a water scale, the Angels would exist as steam and we would be likened to ice. It was the choice of a small number of the six civilisations to slow down their rate of energy frequencies that gave them the ability to experience what it is like to be human.

There is no death, only different levels of being. This statement is the basic truth that underlies all of existence and applies to every different consciousness throughout this universe. Consciousness has been created and cannot be uncreated. Every consciousness, or soul, that exists in the whole of this universe has the right to choose their own state of being. Each choice is made in order to explore all of the opportunities for experience that this universe has to offer.

This universe has been created to allow consciousness the opportunity to freely choose any level and state of existence that can be imagined. There are no limits on personal experience other than that imposed by the individual upon themselves. The whole universe is there to be experienced and all opportunities are available. We have not remembered our origins and the range of available opportunities and have falsely limited our experience and aspirations accordingly. This forgetfulness is not entirely our fault as we have been subject to forces and processes that have limited our view. The time is now right for us to regain our potential and once again travel freely amongst the stars.

Each soul has travelled through many lifetimes and cycles in order to learn and grow. The purpose of creation is to experience. Whatever level of evolution a soul exists at it cannot fulfil its potential during a single lifetime, however long that lifetime is. Each different lifetime allows a different aspect of a soul's potential to be experienced. All of the souls, within this universe have undergone very many cycles of life and we are no exception.

Despite its peculiar and unique energy fields, planet Earth has always been seen as a "physical" paradise. The abundance of life, and the immense joy in that life, has always attracted the many souls of this universe. The planet was always intended to be a place where new experiences could be gained and where creation could be shared with so many diverse forms of life. In some respects planet Earth is the pinnacle of creation and the place where animals and plants could reach new heights of evolution. Mankind was given access to the planet in order to share and enjoy the great joy of creation. Earth was intended to be a place of sharing and growing, a place where all of creation could come and share in its delights and wonders. A place where all could be equal and live in a spiritual and physical harmony. When the members of the six higher civilisations first cloaked themselves in a physical body, this is how life was lived. Nobody saw the world as a place of exploitation or of personal gain, but a world where all of its forms of life lived in harmony and joy.

Each of the "Angels", that came to Earth and lived a human life time, returned to the realms of the six civilisations enriched and invigorated by the experience and encouraged others to experience this form of life for themselves. During the time of Atlantis, very many souls incarnated as human beings and the universe became a better place because of these experiences. Ultimately, because of an unfortunate, but avoidable, accident, Atlantis was lost and, for a time, it appeared as though Earth would be abandoned as a place where individual souls would visit and live. However, the memories of the joys of Earth proved to be too alluring and many of those who had experienced a physical life decided to return and begin a new cycle of human experiences.

When Atlantis was in existence, those who lived a "physical" life were not the same as we are now. Their "physical" bodies were much lighter and of a less dense construction than now. With the arrival of this second group of humans, fully physical bodies were adopted that more closely resembled the forms of matter that animals and plants were constructed of. It was felt that in order to fully experience physical existence, the body's energies should more closely resemble the physical forms of the other planetary life.

Seven physical groups were developed that were each perfectly adapted to their chosen environment and each lived in a separate area of the planet most suited to their chosen form. Each group lived in perfect harmony with each other and all of the planet's other life forms and the planetary consciousness provided all of their minimal material and energy needs. In their turn, the seven groups communicated with and enhanced the planetary consciousness.

The new humans lived comfortably and harmoniously in this way for very many centuries. The changes to this lifestyle, were very slow in occurring and were not fully noticed, by the human population, until it was too late. Although the planetary consciousness was supportive and nurturing towards human life, it was not fully appreciated that the energy frequencies required to maintain planetary and non-human life form stability would have a depleting affect on the human higher brain functions and body metabolism. The frequency of energies, in the form of electro-magnetic waves, could effectively reduce humanity's levels of consciousness to levels not much greater than that of the animals.

The first, and most noticeable loss, were those of higher communication abilities. Humans were, at this time, able to communicate with each other, both within their own groups and across continents, using thought wave transmissions, or psychic means. The planet's dense electro-magnetic wave emissions slowed these functions to an extent where verbal, sound forms of communication needed to be developed. Other functions lost were the abilities of translocation and bi-location, the slowing of the brain capabilities also resulted in the formation of a split between the conscious and the sub-conscious minds, instead of a fully integrated mind, and the body's DNA instruction and memory coding systems being reduced from thirteen strands to only two.

This reduction in higher brain functions considerably reduced mankind's abilities to function as fully as had been intended and there was a danger that individual's levels of consciousness would reduce to a level where they would cease to have any awareness of their origins or their true natures. Several attempts were made by the six higher civilisations to remedy the situation but no lasting solution was found. The only solution was to remove each human, once they had passed out of their physical body and returned to the six, and rescue them from their predicament. Once they had been rescued, they were helped to recover their full capabilities and decide on the next course of action. Human existence was to be continued, but a solution to these problems needed to be found.

In order to generate and support physical forms of life, the planetary consciousness that is Earth, needed to generate energies of a frequency that proved detrimental to the energies that comprise the higher levels of consciousness. If human life was to continue, ways of working with the planet's energy structures needed to be found. The human soul is an immense quantity of energy that is capable of very many levels of existence at the same time. The nature of the energies around Earth compressed these energies to a point where they became dysfunctional. However, in order to live on the planet, humans did not need all of the energy frequencies that comprise the soul. The human soul could be divided into two separate parts, one part to form and motivate the body and another part which could remain separate, but closely connected, which could assist and direct each human through their physical life and the two would be re-united on physical death.

The separate, non-physical aspect of the soul is that which we have come to call the "Higher Self". As each individual was re-born onto the planet, the physical aspect of the soul would drive the physical body and be that part which experienced human life. The second, non-physical aspect would assist the physical soul in maintaining as many elements as possible of the higher brain functions. Gradually, this arrangement began to change and the links between the two aspects of the soul, whilst the individual was living a physical life, began to become restricted and knowledge of the "higher" aspect became reduced.

At this point a new plan was formulated to help mankind regain all of the functions of the soul and be re-united with its true home, the six higher civilisations.

At the start of human existence, each life span had been over 1,000 years. With the reduction in the soul's energies and the other effects of the planet's energy fields, this period had been reduced to approximately 70 years and was not considered a long enough period for humans to experience all that they wish of what the planet had to offer. The plan was that each of us would live a series of lifetimes, as many as the individual chose, in order to gain full experience of the pleasures of human life. The individual would attempt to bring about a raising of the frequencies of the physical aspect of the soul to a level where they could regain full contact with the "higher" aspect and re-unite the two within the physical body.

If the plan did not work fully, the six would intervene and remind mankind of its true place in the universe and its true level of consciousness. The plan has been operating for 7,000 years and it is now time for mankind to re-awaken and regain our full potential. Attempts to re-awaken mankind have been made over the past two hundred years and have had only a limited success. We have appeared to be very reluctant to break away from our physical depths and regain the heights of true awareness.

The choice to re-awaken does not only affect mankind. The planet's consciousness and the life forms that it generates and supports, were at a point where, unless rapid action was taken, the planetary consciousness would not be able to maintain its stability and integrity and would have been in a situation where it could no longer sustain life. The human soul would have continued, whatever happened to the planet, but the soul of the animal and plant life would have disintegrated with that of the planet. There were signs of this occurring in the rapidly increasing number of species that were becoming extinct. These forms of life must be maintained as they exist no where else within creation and their total destruction would not have been allowed to happen. Decisions of this nature are taken on a higher consciousness level and we made our final move in the middle of 1996 thereby bringing about the necessary change.

Fortunately, our time on Earth has not been entirely destructive. The process of re-incarnation has had some very positive effects. Much has been learned about the problems and benefits of life at this high a density of energy. We have never been abandoned to find our own way but have been closely observed and, wherever possible, been helped to take steps along a more enlightening pathway. The six higher civilisations have rarely intervened directly in human affairs, as that would negate the prime directive of freedom of choice, but the occasional hurdle has been cleared and, every once in a while, an idea has been introduced that helped us to a greater understanding of ourselves and our world.

Mankind, as a whole, has moved forwards and has begun to be aware of some of its higher potential and connectedness. The re-incarnation process has allowed mankind to fully experience every aspect of human potential and human frailty. The overcoming of objectives and pre-determined obstacles has meant that we have raised our energy frequencies to a point where re-unification of both aspects of the soul, can begin. As each individual completes their chosen roles in their current lifetime, it frees up many bottlenecks and blocks on memory pathways. This will allow us to remember our roles and past experiences and begin to place these experiences into the larger jigsaw of human existence.

Each person has had a part to play in human evolution and all have now made their own transition out of the karmic cycle. There is no longer any need for suffering or pain, but all should now be preparing to join in the celebrations for the end of the "Human Plan". There will, however, be those souls who have been unable to complete their chosen tasks and are not ready to make their full transition. Many of these souls are leaving the planet and are moving onto other areas of the universe where similar karmic cycles can be experienced. What is important is that these people understand what their lives have meant and their current and, if necessary, past situations have been intended to resolve. Each and every one of us has chosen every major event in our lives for a specific learning process. Once this fact is accepted, by the individual, then all problems cease to be problems but can be seen to be a larger plan for growth. Accept all situations as they arise and all problems will disappear.

Many are reluctant to accept the reality of re-incarnation and this is understandable. The aspect of the soul that forms the physical body is the aspect that re-incarnates. The "Higher" aspect remained apart from the process and the physical aspect did not contain sufficient consciousness to fully remember all of its previous existences. Also, we had set ourselves tasks to accomplish during each incarnation and if the human soul brought full memory of the reasons for completing each task, then we would have tended not to work towards a full completion. Therefore, we have entered into each incarnation with a seemingly blank page with no memory of previous lifetimes. As each person has completed their karmic life cycle, the physical and "higher" aspects of each person's soul begin to re-combine and past life memories begin to filter through into the conscious mind.

We are finally beginning to complete our part of the plan and are slowly becoming aware of our potential. As each person undergoes the re-awakening process, new areas of human potential are being re-discovered. The indicators of the soul's combining are everywhere. Concerns over the planet's and the animal and plant's wellbeing are growing as is a greater understanding of the inter-connectedness of all life. There is a slow acknowledgement of the true make up of the human body and its complex energy structures and with this growth of understanding comes a rejection of "orthodox" medicines and their poisonous chemical treatments. There has been a gradual, but very strong, movement for peace and increasing calls for the destruction of weapons of mass annihilation. It is as though mankind is awakening from a period of only half life and understanding is growing. This does not mean that those who have begun the re-awakening process can become complacent. The word that describes the situation is "beginning". There is very much more work to be completed if humanity, as a whole, is to move forward together.

There is a tendency, amongst those who have begun to re-awaken, to believe that because they have reached a point of greater understanding, that all is well and that they are in a privileged position where they will be "saved" whilst others, who have not achieved the same level of understanding will be left behind. This is not the case. Mankind must move forward together or not at all. Those who have begun to connect with the "higher" aspect of themselves must now begin to help those others to undergo the same awakening.

This is the final act of the karmic cycle, the obligation to help others achieve their own goals and clear the planet of misunderstandings and lack of knowledge. There are no easy routes to our enlightenment and everyone must play their part in bringing the "Human Plan" to completion. This is the completion of the re-incarnation process and all must assist by fulfiling their chosen obligations.

Chapter Three

Pre-Birth and After Death

There is no such thing as coincidence. All events occur for a specific reason and purpose. The reasoning and purpose behind any event occurring is determined by the individuals who are to take part in those events. No event occurs, in an individual's life, that the individual did not plan to happen. This concept is one many of us will have difficulty in accepting. The human world is one where all events are seen as being external, that is imposed upon the individual and that the individual has no control over whether certain events occur or not.

We have become accustomed to seeing our world, and our place in it, in this way and this view is entirely due to the physical aspect of the soul being unable to deal with all of the information, knowledge and experience contained within the whole soul. The human soul is composed of two parts, one part drives the physical body and is that which directly experiences the human cycle of lives and the other part is that which remains apart from the physical and "directs" the activities of the physical whilst it is clothed with a physical body. It has only been when the individual has passed out of the physical that the two parts have been re-united and formed into a "complete" soul. This two aspect situation is now changing. As we are clearing our chosen karmic pathways the two aspects are beginning to combine whilst the individual is still physical and greater understanding of the overall picture is growing.

At the beginning of our karmic history, the "Human Plan", it was necessary to divide human consciousness into two parts. This split was required in order for us to experience physical life whilst retaining as much as possible of overall consciousness. Each person formulated, either individually or in small groups, a planned series of lifetimes that allowed the soul to experience every aspect of potential human experience. As each physical lifetime was lived, a different aspect of physical life could be explored and evaluated for its ability to provide growth, experience and understanding.

The energies that were being emitted by the planetary consciousness, in order to generate and sustain physical life, had proved to be detrimental to human consciousness, as it then existed. The human path has been to work within the planetary consciousness and develop a method of re-combining the two aspects of the human soul so that we, with full consciousness abilities and the higher brain functions, can live as full a life as possible on Earth. The only way to success, in the "Human Plan", was for each individual to live as many lives, within the planetary consciousness energy fields, as possible.

Pre-Birth

It is the purpose of every soul, throughout this universe, to freely choose to experience as much of Creation as possible. The "Human Plan" has used this principle to find a method of working within the planet's electro-magnetic field. All of us have needed to explore, for ourselves, every aspect of human life in order for a full evaluation of method to be completed. Each and every one of us has lived many life times, in as many different ways, to arrive at a complete answer. It has been in this way, and for this reason that each life time has been planned meticulously.

The process of planning began very many years before each life was commenced and involves linking together many individuals and sets of circumstances. The first choice is that of circumstances of birth. Is it to be in a country with a warm climate or one with a cold climate. An "advanced" country or one of more "traditional" life styles. What religious background. A family of wealth, of average means or of poverty. A family where love is abundant and unconditionally given or one where abuse is to occur. Is there to be social rank or one where the family is ostracised. The choices are endless. Every one of us has experienced each and every one of these situations and many more besides.

The next choice is for suitable parents. Generally, but not always, we have formed family groups of individuals who exchange roles, within the group, depending on the experience to be gained. Is it one person's role to be the parent, or another's. Are there areas of genetic irregularities that wish to be experienced that these particular parental genes can supply. How many brothers and sisters are there to be. Will the family live closely or will it spread itself widely. Are there to be any conflicts or just harmony. Is the genetic material that you can supply useful to the family's genetic structures. Whatever choice is made it must fit within the choices made for the circumstances for birth.

Then there is career. Are you to be a wife and mother and not pursue an independent career. Do you wish to climb the social ladder by the type of work done. Will it be a menial job or one of great power. Will your career be creative, such as an artist or musician. Will it be a career where you are unsuccessful but have a strong family to compensate and support you.

Will you be male or female. If female, will you have children and if so, how many. What will their life choices be and how will they connect in with yours. If male, do you act responsibly towards one partner or will you be a philanderer. Will you be gay or lesbian, bi-sexual or heterosexual. What friends will you have. How will they support and help you and how will you interact with them. Are they to share a physical life with you or are they to remain "in spirit" and act as "spirit guides" to help you in your chosen life.

Are any, or all, of these circumstances to be with you for life or will you change them along the way. What additional choices do you put into your life as you are living it. Will the choices be difficult or easy, if difficult, what contingency plans do you make if your courage fails. Is it to be a long, full life or one that is cut short by war or is a murderer to end this life. These particular circumstances are also your choice. Murder occurs because you wish it to or have agreed to it happening in order to satisfy another's wishes.

The list really is endless. Whatever choice can be imagined can be fulfiled and experimented with. Each has lived at least fifty different lives, and sometimes many more. The overriding factors have been choice and the wish for experience. All of these choices are made by the "complete" soul, both "higher" and physical aspects combine to decide on the next life experience.

Each life time can take up to one hundred years to plan to ensure that all of the required individuals and circumstances are able to be in place, ready to act out their part and ensure that all elements come together at the right time. However, the whole planning process takes up only a fraction of the soul's consciousness capabilities. The "higher" aspect of the soul also plans and experiences other areas of evolution and potential whilst the "physical" aspect lives out its plans. This multi-dimensional capability is explored in a later chapter. As can be seen, all of the hard work is completed before an individual is born into their chosen physical life. Human life is there to be enjoyed rather than suffered.

Suffering occurs when the individual attempts to be something that they are not. If all of the planning is to work effectively, the individual has to adopt an attitude of acceptance. Problems have only arisen when the individual has attempted to break away from their planned lives and move into areas where it was not feasible to go. The karmic cycle has been one of learning and growth. When individuals have attempted to stray off their chosen karmic path, this has led to conflict and the concept of karmic debt. Fulfiling karmic debt has been a very time consuming process and has, in overall terms, delayed our progress by at least the span of one life time. Karmic debt re-payment is the main cause of perceived human suffering and is the underlying cause of the recent global situation of increasing personal violence.

We are currently living our last incarnations that are ruled by the karmic cycle of an eye for an eye. There has been a rush to complete these cycles before the cycle changes to one of completion and renewal. The recent global situation would appear to be one of chaos, but it is really only the affects of people clearing out the residue of their individual life plans. The "Human Plan" is completing and as much individual experience as possible needs to be cleared before any leap of consciousness is attempted. Put into this context, current human affairs are actually following a logical route to completion and is not the anarchy that it might appear, on the surface, to be.

After Death

Once an individual's life plan has run its course and all of the chosen areas of exploration have been completed, the physical aspect of the soul returns to its "higher" aspect. The life that has been lived has usually been one where most of the chosen experiences have been undergone and the body's energy reserves begin to be depleted, allowing the soul to release itself from its physical clothes.

The journey to re-unify the soul's aspects is made in several stages. The first feeling is usually one of relief at the release of physical constraints. The second is one of re-uniting with the loved ones who have passed out of the physical during the individual's life time. Over recent years, there have been a number of reports of Near Death Experiences (NDEs) where an individual has undergone the first stages of the return journey. Very often the reports of the NDE has included the arrival of an individual who has taken charge of the person undergoing the NDE, and explained various aspects of what it is the person is experiencing. Identification of this individual is usually coloured by the NDE person's religious beliefs and aspirations. Whatever identity is placed on this individual, the NDE person usually describes them as being unknown but somehow familiar. The new individual is, in fact, the "higher" aspect of the NDE person's soul and usually appears in its "normal" form, that is human in shape, but glowing with an almost blinding white light.

The two aspects of the soul remain totally separate, that is, unmerged. The decision as to whether the two aspects merge is dependant upon the physical aspect's choice of whether further physical experience is required. This decision is made by the physical aspect reviewing its recently completed life and assessing whether it completed its chosen tasks to a satisfactory degree. The life review is carried out by both aspects of the individual's soul, no other parties are involved. Nobody sits in judgement or makes any kind of assessment. Only the individual can judge themselves and choose their next move.

The importance of this reality cannot be stressed too strongly. It is the individual, and only the individual, who can judge their life and the successes and failures made. We have been led to believe that the Creator sits in judgement of an individual's actions, but this is not what actually occurs. No one, not even the Creator, is in a position to judge another, it is only the individual that has that right. Once the soul's review has been completed, further choices are made as to whether the individual remains in "spirit", reincarnates or merges the two aspects of the soul. The decision is made totally by the individual and is determined on the basis of total experience gained and the most appropriate course to be taken to either put the accumulated experience to work or to gain further understanding by one, or more, physical incarnations. As with all aspects of life, throughout this universe, the next situation is one of totally free choice.

If the individual decides to re-incarnate, the procedure detailed under pre-birth is followed. If the individual decides to remain "in spirit", several options are available. The first option is one of a period of rest and reflection. This is carried out with both parts of the soul merged or of the physical aspect resting alone. The period that rest and reflection occupies will vary with each individual and can span a few years or several hundred years. When the individual has considered that they have reflected for long enough, the other options are then re-considered.

To work as a "spirit guide". Most of us are now familiar with the fact that all individuals have several "guides" assisting them in the completion of their individual life plan. "Guides" can be put into, broadly, two categories. There are those who have remained separate from their soul's "higher" aspect and therefore bring only human experience to their role. Some of these "lower guides" are not fully aware of their surroundings and capabilities and can, sometimes, provide more in the way of hindrance than help. However, most are aware of their responsibilities and work closely with the physical individual who has asked them to take on the role of assisting the completion of a life plan. These "guides" tend to have specialist knowledge in certain aspects of human life and the "guides" will vary as the individual they are "guiding" requires such specialist knowledge. For example, the "spirit guide" might have been a medical doctor during one or more physical incarnations and will use this specialised knowledge and experience to help someone who is to work as a doctor or a healer during their current physical life.

All areas of human knowledge and expertise are represented and "guides" are chosen on the basis of their particular field of expertise. The second type of "spirit guide" are those souls who have reached the end of their chosen physical plan and have reached a level of awareness where the two aspects of their soul are able to merge and regain their full level of consciousness. These "guides" tend to work only with physical individuals who are able and prepared to work as mediums as the energy difference between these souls and the incarnate human is usually too great for them to work with "normal" humans. This does not mean that mediums are abnormal, it is just that mediums tend to operate at much higher personal energy frequencies than most people and it is, therefore, usually not possible for these "higher guides" to work with people with "normal" energy levels.

Whereas the human aspect guides will change to suit the prevailing circumstances, in the lives of the physical individuals they are helping, the "higher" level guides will normally work with only one person and stay with that person throughout the whole of that person's physical life. These "higher" guides have tended to adopt a human persona, such as a Chinaman or an American Indian, in order to make their presence more acceptable to those with whom they communicate. This adopted persona is usually chosen from one of the physical incarnations lived by the guide.

The choice of persona is now changing, however, as people become more aware of the presence of "spirit guides" and an increasing number of "channels" are finding that they are beginning to work with guides who adopt no particular human characteristics. The range of options available to those who elect to act as spirit guides are obviously very great and the role is one of considerable responsibility, both to the guide and to the person being guided. However, there is also scope for learning, as the situation chosen by the physical person will also assist the guide in reaching greater understanding of the human condition. The last option is to return to the six civilisations, or as we would term it, heaven. This option is only available to those souls who have merged both physical and higher aspects of their soul and have decided that their part of the "Human Plan" has been completed.

The journey back also involves a period of rest and reflection in order to ensure that the individual is certain that this is the best option. It also allows the individual a period to remove any final undesirable elements of human characteristics. The memory of this period is that which has given rise to the religious concept of only the "pure of heart" being able to enter heaven. This particular option has not been chosen by very many people as the "Human Plan" is seen as being of great significance and virtually all of those involved have opted to remain close to the planet. When this option is finally taken, it once again opens up the whole of the universe to the individual for exploration and new experience.

The areas and options, that have been discussed in this chapter, are only to highlight the main areas of our choice. In reality, the choices that have been available have been limited only by the individual's imagination and wish for experience. As we live out the final acts of the "Human Plan", these available options are changing. The re-incarnation, karmic cycle has come to its end. Human conflict is set to totally cease and a "New Age" of understanding and enlightenment is dawning. The universal energies, that promote re-newal and change are coming to bear fully on the planet. Earth is currently bathed in an energy that has not been experienced, by this area of the galaxy, for over twenty thousand years.

The ending of the "Human Plan" was timed to coincide with the arrival of these energies and it is time for humanity to shake off their physical constraints and rejoin the rest of the universal community.

Chapter Four

Sexuality

Every soul is truly androgynous, each is both male and female, but also neither. This means that the subject of sexuality is uniquely human. Of all the choices to be made, to finalise the pre-birth plan, the most important, and most far reaching choice, is that of sexual identity. The choice of sexuality is one which pervades all areas of life and determines the availability of many areas of our experience.

Sex is an energy that is made up of frequencies that can be expressed in terms of being either male or female, homosexual or heterosexual. The male and female aspects are required, primarily, to make physical reproduction possible, but also to allow for the capacity to experience the variety of emotional and situational differences that are only possible by being either male or female. Whatever sex an individual is, in this lifetime, it should be remembered that they have been of the opposite sex in several previous lifetimes.

It should also be remembered that no person is entirely male or entirely female, both sexes have elements of the other as part of their make up. In males, female energies express themselves as emotions and insecurities. In females, the male energies express themselves as desire and the aggression to protect their offspring. The true human condition is one of balance, between the two energies, which is currently finding expression in the growing number of people who consider themselves to be genderless, the group that is calling themselves the "Third Gender". It is also through sexuality, and the sexual act, that the physical soul finds a particular form of expression and a means of connection to its "higher" aspect.

Sex is an activity in which, virtually, all of us overindulge. It is seen as a right and a necessary part of our physical and emotional well being. There is a tendency to place an overemphasis on this activity and give it a greater importance than is entirely necessary. Our bodies are intended, and in fact designed, to gain pleasure from the close, physical contact from another person, whether this contact is overtly sexual or not. Sexual activity adds another dimension to this enjoyment and can, unfortunately, in some instances, lead to a form of addiction.

At the start of human existence, the sexual act was considered sacred. The union was seen as being not only that of two bodies but also of two souls. The frequencies at which we then existed meant that the sexual act, particularly at the point of climax, unified the two souls to a point where, for that brief period, they were joined together at a frequency that connected the two souls with the "universal soul", which can also be a direct connection with the Creator. As our frequencies reduced, and became more physical, this connection with the "universal soul" has lessened and emotional, physical connections have taken over. This does not mean to say that the "higher" frequency connections are not possible, they are just more difficult to attain.

All of the life forms throughout all of Creation, form bonds with other life forms that are at a compatible energy frequency. With us, this energy compatibility is called love. Love is not necessarily expressed in sexual terms, even though it very often is, but is the basis for all of our relationships, be they sexual or platonic, male or female.

Physical, sexual desire for another human being is only one aspect of the frequency of the energies known as love. However, it is the primary aspect and one which serves the purpose of producing offspring that also have an energy frequency that is compatible with both parents. This compatibility is extremely important as, without it, humanity begins to disintegrate and degenerate into dysfunctional family groups where there is no harmony between the parents and the child.

It has been mentioned that there are "physical souls" who are not fully aware of themselves or their surroundings. These souls tend to be individuals who have removed themselves from the overall "Human Plan" in order to pursue lives of purely physical pleasure without regard to the consequences or for their own progression. When these souls pass out of the physical, their only intent is to return to a physical life as quickly as possible. They therefore search out those incarnate souls who are of a like frequency and thought and can, in certain circumstances, impose their choice, for a new life, on one, or both, parents. In this way some people have formed themselves into small groups who constantly re-cycle themselves purely in pursuit of physical, mainly sexual, pleasures. For these people, life, and its purposes, is totally misunderstood and they use sex and sexuality as a means of making their lives meaningful. Fortunately, the number of these groups is very small and they have had a very limited affect on overall human progression. Never the less, this group has been able to generate, within the human mass consciousness, a feeling of confusion and fear greatly disproportionate to their numbers which has led, during some periods of our history, to a feeling of non-specific discomfort amongst other areas of the population.

As we are, currently, undergoing a period of change and transition, all of the dis-incarnate souls of this group are being encouraged to move to other areas of the universe, away from Earth, where they can be helped to re-direct their energies and arrive at a greater understanding, thereby eliminating their disruptive affects to themselves and to mankind as a whole.

As human consciousness reduced, sex and sexuality changed and we began to use our sexuality in different ways and, very often, as a means of gaining control over others. The choice of being born either male or female is one which is made in order to experience aspects of human existence that can only be experienced by being of that particular sex. Within this choice there is also an opportunity for expression of aspects of an individual's total consciousness. This form of expression manifests itself in very many different ways and is usually chosen as a means of educating others by illuminating flaws in stereotypical attitudes. An example of this would be an extremely aggressive woman or a very emotional and sensitive man. Both examples show the extreme ranges of human experience which serve to remind us that each sex is composed of a range of elements of the other and that all can be accommodated within individuals and by society at large.

At the start of the twentieth century, Earth entered an area of the universe where energies for change are available. These energies have manifested themselves in many different ways, but the most important has been the breakdown of stereotypical roles, for the sexes, that have developed over many centuries. In order to re-build, there first has to be a dismantling of the old.

Human society has, over most of its history, fallen into the trap of repression and elitism. Much of this repression has followed sexual divisions. For the past few centuries it is men who have repressed women, but, up until 4,000 years ago, it was women who held power. Whichever sex has been in control, they have always misunderstood their roles and responsibilities. Both men and women have had an equal part to play in human development but one role has always seemed more appealing, and therefore more powerful, than the other, with both aspects of the power struggle using sexuality as the basis for the repression of the other. As we became more physical, and therefore more human, it was women who were seen as being the dominant sex. Women have always been more sensitive and nurturing than men and, having the ability to control their bodies for reproduction, were perceived as having control over life. As women had control over new life they were seen as being of a closer connection to the Creator than men and should, therefore, be closely protected and given control over all aspects of life. This attitude produced the principle of Mother Earth, or Gaia, and the many goddess religions and fertility rites based around female statuary.

With the advent of financially based trade, which was controlled almost exclusively by men, men gradually began to see themselves as the providers and, therefore, the rightful holders of power. This led to a struggle between the sexes that has been mirrored in the women's movement of the past thirty years. The difference now is that women are fighting for equality, a bringing into balance, whereas 4,000 years ago, men were fighting for domination.

The overwhelming desire for control led to a denial of the responsibilities that accompany this level of power which has led men into a form of megalomania that has taken 3,000 years to remedy. The conquest of female power has led to the repression of both sexes and a great deal of confusion in human understanding. Women have never sought power, only balance, the power had been given to them by men who had not understood the strength and power of an equal partnership. There have been two influences on human history that have shaped humanity more than any others. The first was the effects of the planet's electro-magnetic wave frequencies and the second was the sexual revolution that led to male domination. Both have had an equally devastating affect on human development and understanding.

There was not anything wrong with men wishing to remove the power from women as it should have led to a situation where both assumed their most suited roles in the sharing of responsibility for life. The problems arose when men overstepped their intentions and physically took control over women leading to an assumption of domination and the maintaining of that domination. There are some genetic groups which have maintained the correct balance of respect for the appropriate roles for each of the sexes, but for most, male domination has, until recently, been accepted as the norm.

The main weapon used by men has been the bodily functions that gave women their power in the first place : the ability to produce and nurture new life. By using this basic biological fact against women, men have been able to repress women and maintain a position of power. Women have always been able to control the cycle of ovulation and, therefore, be in total control of the physical aspects of the child birth process. Although the birth of a child is by agreement with the three souls involved, it is women who have always been in a position to control whether conception occurred or not. Constant repression and lack of understanding by men, has led women to forget this elementary fact and they have effectively given most of their power away. This situation has led to a constant sexual repression where moral values have been male dominated and given rise to all of the contradictions and conflict of values that have resulted from the lack of shared responsibilities. It was only with the introduction of effective contraceptives that women could regain control of their bodies and break the male domination cycle. The contraceptive pill allowed human sexuality to change and bring about a situation where a regaining of the correct balance was possible.

The shift of energies has been enormous and is a major factor in allowing the transitionary process to fully proceed. How could mankind move forwards if half of the population was not allowed its full share of responsibility. This does not mean that men are beyond redemption, nor does it mean that they are entirely to blame for this situation. Although men desired power, it was women who allowed them to take it and then continued to accept their repression.

The area of human sexuality is one which is extremely complex and the range of choices is as diverse as the number of individuals who are living a physical life. The only "normal" aspect of a heterosexual relationship is that it allows for the possibility of producing offspring. Other forms of expression, and therefore sexual preference, have always existed. Whatever choice an individual soul makes, it is based on the areas that have been explored in the past, allowing for a new area of exploration and expression in the present. All individuals have changed their sex, and sexual preferences, to suit their desired life plan for each successive life time. Nobody has lived all of their lives as the same sex. However, many successive life times as one sex can lead to some level of identity confusion when the choice is made to live as the opposite sex in the next life time. This level and form of confusion is responsible for a very small percentage of people who live as bi-sexuals, trans-sexuals and homosexuals. However, the vast majority of people who express their sexuality in these ways have specifically chosen to do so.

There are many people who are of the opinion that single sex preference is some kind of dis-function or genetic abnormality, but this is not the case. The choice of sexuality is one which is freely and deliberately made as a means of expression, experience and, in some instances, as a way of teaching others that prejudices are not justified. Prejudice only occurs when one group of people feels threatened by another and the perceived threat is a consequence of the first group being very insecure in their own belief systems. The group that is prejudiced against will, in their turn, feel threatened by the other group's insecurities and areas of conflict arise. If each group acknowledges the right of the other to choose their identities and lifestyles, conflict and aggression becomes totally unnecessary. As with all areas of human life, false moral values need to be removed and a correct balance of understanding reached. This is why homosexual groups have striven for acceptance during this century, as it is a means of education to help break down unwarranted sociological barriers and prejudices derived from major sexual insecurities. Each person is who they have chosen to be. Problems only arise when a person attempts to become someone they are not.

As the new millenium approaches, and the opportunity for our transformation has arrived, many of those born in the last half of the twentieth century have brought with them a new form of sexual expression. The growing group of people that have called themselves "The Third Gender" are helping mankind to understand that the balance of male/female energies and sexual activity is not incompatible. This does not make them freaks, but the first true humans to arrive on the planet since the commencement of the "Human Plan".

We have become so totally engrossed in the physical differences between men and women that we have difficulty in recognising the similarities. The individuals, who comprise the third gender group, are those who have recognised the balance and symmetry of the human soul and have chosen to acknowledge this state of balance by presenting themselves as being not overtly sexual in either guise. What they are attempting to show mankind is that, on a consciousness, or soul level, all are the same and that there should not be conflict between the sexes but only harmony and respect.

The time for the cessation of all conflict is rapidly approaching, but it can only be successfully achieved if there is complete understanding. Without examples of what balance and harmony is, it would be difficult for mankind to understand. These "genderless" individuals have chosen to take on the role of teachers to help mankind to see that human sexuality is really only a fabricated veneer that served a specific purpose.

The time has arrived when all false values, misunderstandings and misconceptions can be removed and humanity can move forwards with understanding and enlightenment.

Chapter Five

Channelling

Channelling is a term that has come into common usage in recent years and is one with which many people will still be unfamiliar. The term applies to a person who is able to allow certain forms of energy to be connected with their own, personal energy systems for the purpose of communication. Most people will be familiar with the terms clairvoyant, clairaudient, clairsentient, mediums and spiritual healers (those who practice what used to be called the laying on of hands and faith healing). All of these practitioners have agreed to allow themselves to be used as a "channel" for energies that are beneficial to mankind. Whether this benefit is to help understand aspects of their life, past, present or future, or by a healer re-balancing the energies within the body to remedy an illness. All of the energy workers can be included under the umbrella term of channeller.

The process of channelling works in two ways, both of which are applicable to all channellers. The first is an ability to consciously receive communications from the channeller's "spirit guides" and the second is an ability to connect with what is popularly known as the "Higher Self". The term "higher self", as most people interpret it, is a misnoma and a misunderstanding of the make up of the human soul. The soul, in its normal state, is an immense quantity of energy. In order to live a physical life, with all of the limitations that that state imposes, it is not possible for all of the soul's energy to enter this limited space. Therefore certain aspects, of an individual's soul, remain outside of, but fully connected to, that part which forms the physical. The "Higher Self", therefore, is not a separate part of the individual, as most people have interpreted the term, but is a fully connected and fully functioning part of the individual.

When a person connects with their higher self, what they have actually achieved is a clearing of some of the energy pathways, within the soul, and allowed the energy to flow more freely. It is like when we put pressure on a part of our anatomy, the blood ceases to flow and parts of our anatomy lose feeling. If the pressure is removed, the blood begins to flow again and feeling returns. Most people live their lives with pressure on the energy connections within the soul, and this is why, for those who have found ways of easing this pressure, the return of the connection feels so enlightening.

Channelling exists in an infinite variety of forms, many of which would not normally be recognised as channelling. However, we have given names to recognised forms of channelling and it would be easier to start with a description of these.

Clairvoyance

The term clairvoyance is usually used as a generic term that includes other terms such as clairaudience and clairsentience. Clairvoyance is defined as a person having the ability to literally see their, or other people's, "spirit guides" and communicate with them. Clairaudience is an ability to hear the guides but without the ability to see them. Clairsentience is an ability to sense the presence of the guides but without the ability to see or hear them directly.

Effectively, these three abilities amount to the same thing: an ability to communicate with those who are no longer physical. This is an ability that all of us have. It is only the preparedness, of the individual, to allow themselves to be used as a communication channel that makes one person clairvoyant and not another. The way in which this form of communication works is that the "spirit guide" comes close to the clairvoyant and the frequency of the clairvoyant's energies are altered to bring them closer to that of the "spirit". Communication takes place by the "guide" transmitting energy patterns, to the clairvoyant, which sets in motion a series of resonances within the clairvoyant's body. The body's neural systems respond to the energy resonances and transmit this response to the sub-conscious mind. The sub-conscious sorts out the neural signals and responds by activating sensory centres within the conscious mind allowing the clairvoyant to see, hear or sense the message.

The clairvoyant communicates their part of the conversation by forming the questions, responses etc., in the conscious mind. This is then transferred, from the conscious mind, to the areas of the brain where there are thought wave transmitter centres located and transmitted to the "spirit" they are conversing with. This sounds like a complicated, time consuming, process but in fact it is quicker than the process required for two people to hold a conversation using normal speech. It is well within the capabilities of all of us to receive communications in this way and virtually all instances of "inspiration" are clairvoyant communications. One of the main criticisms of clairvoyant communications is their seeming inaccuracies. There are several reasons for this.

The clairvoyant might put their own interpretation onto the message and, therefore, alter it to suit their own viewpoint. The person receiving the message might put their own interpretation onto the message and alter their understanding of it to suit their wished for interpretation. By far the most common reason for apparent inaccuracies is the fact that each and every individual has full freedom of choice and the prediction of future events depends on each element of that prediction following a probable course of action. If one of the individuals, involved in a predicted event, chooses to take a course of action that is not part of the most likely course, then the probability of the event occurring, as predicted, is altered. Despite these factors, many clairvoyants do in fact achieve an accuracy in excess of 90%. This is achieved by the clairvoyant putting their personal viewpoints to one side and allowing the full message to be given without interpretation.

Mediums

Mediumship and clairvoyance are totally different processes and one where the potential pitfalls of clairvoyance can be avoided. Mediumship has a history at least as long as that of clairvoyance and has suffered from the same misunderstandings and denunciations based on fear and the loss of power. In clairvoyance, the channel is in two way communication with the spirit guides and passes messages to and from the questioner.

A medium, on the other hand, allows the spirit guide to use their mind and vocal chords to talk directly with the questioner and it is the questioner who communicates directly with the spirit guide. This means of communication is only possible if the channel and the spirit guide have total trust in one another.

Traditionally, the process involved is that the medium allows their consciousness to be temporarily "displaced" and the vacated "space" filled by the "spirit guide". This type of medium is usually called a trance medium because of this letting go. The medium does not actually enter a trance state, it just appears that way. The medium's consciousness does not actually go anywhere but is "switched off" and it is for this reason that mediums do not remember any of the messages that are transmitted through them. To allow the loss of consciousness, in this way, takes a great act of courage by the medium and there are not many people who are prepared to act in this way any more and the number of trance mediums is diminishing.

The main advantage, of this form of communication, is that there is no re-interpretation of the message by the channel. In recent years, mediumship has begun to change and the channelling process has become, increasingly, one of co-operation rather than one of letting go. Modern mediums are now much more aware of what is happening and the message that is being conveyed.

Spiritual Healers

Healers also channel energies and with this energy, very often, come messages. Healers allow themselves to be the channel for particular frequencies of energy that correspond to human physical frequencies. The human body is composed and manufactured from energy that takes the form of highly compacted energy vortices that combine together to form the atomic and molecular structures. The form that these molecular structures build into is controlled by a combination of the DNA memory structures, informing each molecule what its function is, and the soul, or consciousness, informing each molecule of its specific location within the body.

As consciousness enters the body that it has constructed for itself, it brings with it the life force that drives the body. This life force combines with all of the body's molecular structures and also forms the link between the "physical" element of the soul and the "higher" element of the soul. The energy contained within the life force also creates centres of energy, mainly located along the spine, that have become known as "Chakras". Chakra is a Hindu word that means "spinning wheel" which describes the appearance of the chakra when it is functioning correctly.

Each chakra has a particular frequency that corresponds to certain regions of the physical body. The energy, from the chakras, is distributed around the corresponding areas of the body through a network of meridians. These meridians are criss-crossed throughout the body and carry energy to all areas of the body. Where the meridians cross each other they form miniature chakras that are the acupuncture points.

The human body's chakra and meridian systems have a direct correlation in the planet's ley line network. There are seven chakras contained within the physical body and each chakra has a particular frequency that gives it a specific colour.

The first chakra, the base or root chakra, is located at the base of the spine and is defined as the chakra that governs understanding of the physical dimensions and "roots" the individual in the physical. It is the energy centre through which we experience the "fight or flight" response. It is related to the adrenal gland and controls the functions of the kidneys and the spinal column. It is coloured red.

The second chakra is located in the sexual organs - ovaries in women and the testes in men. It is the chakra relating to creativity. It governs attitudes in relationships, sex and reproduction. It is coloured orange.

The third chakra is located in the solar plexus. It is connected to the liver, spleen, stomach, gall bladder and some aspects of the nervous system. It also relates to the pancreas. It is the area of the body that deals with emotional issues and personal power. It is coloured yellow.

The fourth chakra is the heart chakra. It is connected to the heart, blood and circulatory system, the immune system and the endocrine system. It also influences the thymus gland. This is the connecting point for the lower "physical" energies and the higher "spiritual" energies and this is why it is the centre through which love is felt. It is coloured green.

The fifth chakra is in the throat, just above the adams apple, and is associated with the thyroid gland. It is connected to the lungs, vocal chords, bronchial channels and the metabolism. It is the area that deals with communication, expression and judgement. It is coloured blue.

The sixth chakra is located in the third eye, in the centre of the forehead, and is associated with the pituitary gland. It controls the lower brain and the nervous system, the ears, nose and the left eye. This is the centre of our spirituality. It is coloured indigo.

The seventh chakra, or crown chakra, is the top of the head and is associated with the pineal gland. It controls the upper brain and the right eye. This is the entry point for the higher "spiritual" energies. Its colour depends upon the frequency of the individual and is at its "lowest" with the colour violet, or a mixture of all colours as white, or at its "highest" with the colour gold.

There are six other chakras beyond these seven that extend very far out into the universe. These do not have a colour and are related to the "higher" consciousness and connections to the "universal" soul. These six, non physical chakras are, as yet, largely unknown to us, but they will gain in significance as we undergo our transitions.

The process of integrating the two parts of our consciousness is achieved by utilising the six "higher" chakras. In January 1997 each individual's "higher self" began altering the energies contained within each person. The chakras began to spin faster and extend further out from the body. At the same time, the six higher chakras overlaid the six lower chakras within the body, the crown remains open and largely unaltered, and when each individual's personal energy system has expanded sufficiently, they will connect with the higher chakras and begin to draw the higher frequencies into the physical body. The effect this will have is to raise each person's frequency levels so that they can begin to absorb the higher self into the sub-conscious mind. The process will continue throughout 1997 and into 1998.

When complete, this will allow each person to have access to the full range of their memories and understanding. The view of the world changes as this process continues and many things that have been considered important lose their significance and areas which have not been considered before take on a greater importance. The hard work necessary to allow this process to happen has already been completed by each individual before the end of 1996. All that is now required is to sit back and enjoy the experience.

As can be seen, we are much more of an energy being than is traditionally supposed. The body cannot be viewed as a collection of separate organs, but is a masterpiece of light that glows and sparkles when its energies are correctly balanced. Illness and disease is caused when the energies become imbalanced over a prolonged period. The main area where imbalance is created is the solar plexus chakra. We are extremely emotional and tend to carry round emotional hurts for many years. Considering how emotional we are, it is surprising that we have not yet learnt how to deal with them properly or how to clear out emotional imbalances.

The healers work by allowing their bodies to become channels for energies that are mainly brought through the non-physical chakras and the higher consciousness and brought through their bodies and out through their hands. The energy flows out through one hand and is taken back through the other hand to complete an energy "circuit". Each healer has their own way of working and some will experience the energy flow through the left hand and some through the right hand.

The healer, when working with a patient, allows this energy to flow into the patient's body by placing their hands about 1"-2" (25-50mm) away from the patient's body. The energy flow will tend to find its own way to the areas of the patient's body that most require healing. This is healing in its most basic form and how all healer's operate. There are very many levels above this that vary depending on the abilities of the healer and the requirements of the patient. Very often, specialist "guides" will work with a healer and will take over the work of the healing once the healer has begun the healing process.

Any physical illness can be healed in this way. The determining factor, of how effective a healing is, is dependant upon the patient. All illnesses are self induced, by one means or another, and the patient needs to learn what it is in their make up that triggered the imbalance in the first place. If the patient can deal with the root cause of the problem, then the illness can be fully healed, by the healer. However, if the patient is not prepared to help themselves, then the healer will only be able to relieve the symptoms and not fully heal the problem.

These methods of channelling were developed and have evolved in response to our needs. As needs have changed so have forms of channelling. As we enter a new phase of evolution forms of channelling are also evolving to suit our varying needs. The first changes that are occurring will be noticed mainly by clairvoyants and mediums, many of whom will have already noticed a subtle shift in energy patterns. Healing energies are also changing, but not as quickly. However, many healers will have noticed an increase in the number of patients asking for healing and a proportionately higher success rate.

We have, even on passing over from the physical, always tended to stay closely connected with the planet and have, on many occasions, had an influence on the lives of those still physical. Very often this influence has not been particularly helpful and sometimes very disruptive. What we now require is a period of positive assistance and, therefore, many of the individuals, who are pre-disposed to interference, are being persuaded away from the planet and to travel to areas of the universe where assistance and education can more readily be provided. A number of clairvoyants and mediums will have already noticed a more positive energy, a lightening of spirit, of those with whom they deal because of the removal of these disruptive energies.

Within the range of options that an individual has, as part of their free choice of level of existence, is one of remaining in "spirit" and providing positive help and guidance to those who choose further physical lifetimes. There are a number of individuals who have lived several physical lifetimes and achieved a high level of existence and understanding, who have chosen to remain in spirit. These individuals will, very often, adopt a persona of a favoured previous physical life, such as a Native American or a Chinaman, and seek out physical individuals with whom they can work as "guides". These are the individuals with whom most clairvoyants and mediums have traditionally dealt.

These relationships will continue, where both the "guide" and the guided wish them to, but many mediums, in particular, will notice that their "guides" will begin to change and they will be contacted by "entities" who have not lived a previous human life or who have lived on Earth, but have moved on to other areas of the universe before electing to return to Earth to provide assistance at this time. This can prove to be an interesting and enlightening experience for both the medium and the visiting "entity" and both can learn a great deal from each other. There will also be a number of mediums who will be in contact with those in the higher frequencies of the six civilisations, the "Angels". For these mediums, the experience will be a little different. Direct contact, between the medium and the six, will not always be possible, due to the immense differences in energy frequencies. The communications will be relayed through one, or more, "entities" who will act as energy transformers, stepping down the energies of the link in order for the medium to receive them. These intermediaries will not alter the messages or interfere in any way, there is no such thing as ego amongst the Angels. Their role is purely to act as relay stations to allow two way communications between the medium and the Angel.

As with all forms of channelled communications, there should be a note of caution. There are many entities travelling to our solar system, at this time, who wish to be available to assist us through our transitionary phase. Many of these entities are well meaning but lack many areas of information. These entities are in communication with a number of people and the messages that they convey, whilst not necessarily wrong, do not contain the whole truth and contain many inaccuracies and predictions of events which have a very low probability of occurring.

It cannot be said that these entities should not be communicated with, but their messages should be treated with caution. The medium should satisfy themselves that they are acting with the best of intentions and actively search for the truth, in all situations, before trying to present communications from these entities as being accurate. Readers of such communications should look to see if what they are reading resonates with their own truth and reject those communications that do not "feel" correct.

As with all things, truth has an energy which creates a resonance within the individual. Whilst every person has their own truth and their own reality, if the writings do not resonate with that person, then they should be rejected. The same applies to these writings. An attempt has been made, on these pages, to present an accurate portrayal of events in our past. If as an individual, you do not recognise a truth that is acceptable, then reject all or part of this book and continue with your own personal search for a truth that is found to be acceptable. What is important is that you do begin your search and do not rely on others to find the truth for you.

There are no absolute rules any longer, neither are there any easy answers. Each individual must make up their own mind and find their own truth. The individual has total responsibility for themselves.

What lies in the near future for channelling, is really a return of some of the higher brain functions that relate to psychic forms of communication. As the planet moves into direct alignment with the area of potential energies, most of us will find that, even if we have never experienced channelling before, we will be able to communicate directly with our guides. Those who already work as clairvoyants and mediums will find new areas of communication opening up. The most noticeable, and probably most fascinating for those involved, will be the ability to communicate psychically with other clairvoyants and mediums as a forerunner to all people re-discovering this ability. In this way we will, for the first time in many centuries, be able to fully communicate our thoughts and feelings to those around us. No more misunderstandings or misinterpretations, real or imagined, so there will be no excuses for hostilities or subterfuge.

All of us have these abilities, and many more, already encoded in our DNA and locked away in our sub-conscious minds. It now only requires the genuine desire for these and other latent abilities to be unlocked and once again made available to all of us. Each and every person is alive, at this time, to take advantage of this opportunity for change. This opportunity will not arise again for another 20,000 years. Do not be afraid to make the first step.

It is only the individual who has the right to choose whether they fulfil their potential or not.

Chapter Six

Multidimensionality

There is one aspect of consciousness that encompasses all others. The human body, as it normally exists, is not capable of accepting the whole of the soul's energies. Only about 10-15% of the total consciousness actually comprises the "physical" soul. The percentage is approximate and obviously varies from individual to individual. Ten percent is roughly the quantity of consciousness that is required to drive the human adult body and perform the basic functions required to live a "normal" human lifetime. More "advanced" people, those who have progressed some way along their personal journey to understanding and completion, usually have integrated no more than about 30% of their overall consciousness whilst still physical.

The main reason for these individuals not exceeding 30% is that if they had integrated a higher percentage, they would literally shine out from the crowd and probably would have been the basis for new religions. The situation is now rapidly changing and a growing number of people, who have completed their personal part of the "Human Plan", are beginning to be able to integrate far higher percentages than has previously been possible. These individuals do actually shine out from the crowd but because mankind, as a whole, is progressively integrating more consciousness, these individuals do not have the "beacon" effect that they would have had previously. There are, in fact, some individuals who have accumulated up to 75% of their total consciousness. The average, however, remains at around 30%. The intention of the "Human Plan" is to fully integrate 100% of consciousness into the physical body and is the purpose of the current state of change. The transitionary energies, now available, are capable of helping us, for the first time in 15,000 years, into becoming fully functioning beings.

But, if our existence only requires as low a percentage as 10% to function "normally", what does the remainder of our consciousness do whilst the 10% is physical? Of all answers and concepts discussed in this book, the answer to this question is one which many will find the most difficult to accept. In theory, the whole human consciousness could actually produce ten different individual "physical souls" at the same time.

This condition has not actually occurred but, never the less, it has been a real possibility. What that would actually mean is ten different versions of the same person living a physical life all at the same time. It would, however, be true to say that the consciousness, of which each human physical soul is a small percentage, does explore other possibilities, other experiences, as other living physical entities at the same time as a human life is lived. This, to many people, would appear to be a statement of the impossible. Never the less, it is a fact. As our abilities to integrate total consciousness increase, a growing number of people are becoming aware of this region of a soul's journeyings and the reality is slowly being accepted.

The origins of the consciousness energy, of which humans are comprised, is the realms of the six higher civilisations, who were created to explore and experience. In the process of creation the Creator brought into being individual consciousnesses, or souls, that reflect the Creator's make up, but at a smaller scale. Effectively, the Creator created a multi-purpose being that is capable of existing at many levels of energy frequency and many states of consciousness at the same time. Virtually all of the individuals, who comprise the six higher civilisations, remain as a single consciousness, however, they retain the capacity for multidimensional existences.

When the Creator requested "volunteers" to explore planet Earth, it was anticipated that the whole consciousness could exist at human physical energy frequencies. With the realisation that this was not the case, came the formulation of the "Human Plan" and the multidimensional capabilities were made use of. As the planning of the "Human Plan" was being completed, it was realised that the 7,000 years that were available was not a long enough period for the whole of the potential experience that this new level of life offered, to be experienced. The total time span only allowed for a maximum of seventy human lifetimes to be lived and it became increasingly clear that one, or more, concurrent lives needed to be lived. There are no limits to experience availability. If something is available, the soul or consciousness, has the capacity to experience it. This is true for all aspects of the universe and is certainly true for all areas of life on Earth.

All things that have been created have a consciousness and it shares that consciousness with the Creator. From the smallest bacteria through to plants and animals, planets, stars, galaxies and up to the universe itself, all have a consciousness of some form, a soul, that links it to the Creator. Each of these souls is capable of, or is a part of, a multidimensional existence. Our planet is a consciousness that comprises a part of the solar system consciousness and the solar system consciousness is a part of the galactic consciousness. The same is true for human consciousness. A percentage of the remaining total consciousness also forms about itself another physical form and lives a separate existence to that of the percentage consciousness that is reading this book. In other words, each individual is one part of a twin, or triplets, or more, each living their own lives and totally unaware of the existence of the others.

The whole process is, of course, different for each individual soul and depends entirely on that soul's individual plans and wishes for particular experiences. There are no hard and fast rules, only the choices of the individual.

There is no need for us to develop a complex over this reality. The concept will be very new and probably quite daunting to many people. The whole process has existed since the advent of the "Human Plan" and there has been no need for the separate elements to be aware of each other until the time for full integration was at hand. As with reincarnation, we would spend most of our time investigating the other elements of self instead of living our planned life, therefore, full knowledge of the extent of human capability would have been counter-productive.

If each of us had full awareness of these facts, humanity would be no further forward than it was 7,000 years ago. Full integration of the soul is now happening for most people and the full story of human capability and history is beginning to emerge. Awareness of the full capabilities of our souls must be made available in order for individuals to make full sense of their awakening memories.

The range of experience available to us is very considerable and it would not have been possible for one percentage aspect of an individual's soul to cover all of these possible areas during the allotted time period. Each human lifetime can take up to one hundred years to plan and then up to one hundred years to live out. Successive generations create new areas of possibility and there have, therefore, always been new areas of life to explore. The process could have been, theoretically, never ending and a way needed to be found to allow all individuals as free a choice of experience as possible. The only way was for each individual to live more than one reincarnation cycle at a time by portioning the total consciousness into "physical soul" pieces. In order for the scheme to work effectively each "portion", of the total consciousness, would choose a life so that there was no possibility for the separate parts, or friends or relatives etc., to meet. This has meant an immense amount of careful planning and has been, on the whole, very successful.

So how does this system work? The purpose of human life is to explore all of the possibilities and experiences that life, at this high a density, has to offer whilst exploring ways of allowing for the possibility of fully integrating the whole consciousness into a human body and function within the planet's electro-magnetic field. This has been the "Human Plan".

There are three main areas of life that determine a person's experience of life. These are: the person's sex, the person's financial status and the person's connectedness with the planetary consciousness. These three areas determine the individual's life and the experiences that they are able to gain. All three can be explored separately or a life can be planned that incorporates one, two or all of these elements. The possible combinations are, obviously, endless. The total consciousness is split into two, or more, physical consciousnesses and collectively they work out a series of personal plans that each "physical" soul is to explore in a series of lifetimes. These lifetimes might coincide with each other or they may overlap or only one "physical" soul might be living a physical life at any one time. However these separate lifetimes have been lived, they have allowed for the full spectrum of human experience to be explored.

Examples of these separate lives might be:

"Soul One": a successful businessman living in, say, Madrid. This life would explore how a position of wealth and power could be dealt with. Should the person be kind and generous or mean and cruel? How does either approach affect the other people around him? Is having wealth and power a positive or a negative benefit? Would the situation be enhanced if there was a spiritual element or would a more ecological approach be appropriate?

"Soul Two": a woman living within an isolated tribal culture, say Papua New Guinea. Are women of greater, equal or less value than men in such a tribal culture? Could the tribal structure and traditions be altered in certain ways to improve the tribal well being? How is child bearing dealt with? Could it be improved? Does a closer connection with the planetary consciousness help in understanding the world around the tribe?

"Soul Three": a man struggling for financial survival within a major city, say Tokyo. This life would explore how a lack of wealth and social standing is perceived. Does financial wealth really make a big difference to life? Would the human experience be better served if there was no monetary systems? Does the lack of money allow a person to be closer to nature and the planetary consciousness?

These would be examples for a form of existence lived in one incarnation. For the next, or subsequent incarnation, the choices might be to look at the opposite possibilities.

"Soul One": a penniless woman living on the streets of Madrid. Which is the most effective way to live? Is wealth and power of greater benefit than being destitute? Is discrimination against this type of person justified or is it as a result of others fearing being in the same situation themselves? Is there more opportunity to investigate human existence by being homeless or rich? How do attitudes to both types of people vary within the same culture?

"Soul Two": a middle income housewife living in say, Minnesota. Are "Western" values a better option than tribal values? Is there more scope for understanding and expansion where material goods are more readily available? Is childbirth better dealt with by tribal customs or contemporary medicines? How do male values differ between both cultures? Is the role of a woman valued more or less?

"Soul Three": a woman of great wealth living in say, London. Are the perceptions of wealth different for a woman or a man? Are there advantages to either sex in either situation? Can a woman deal with the pressures of wealth better or worse than a man? Does privilege and wealth help us achieve a greater understanding of ourselves and our world?

These scenarios are given as an example of the types of exploration undertaken by the "physical" soul in trying to determine the best and the worst that a human society is capable of. The choices illustrated could apply to any time throughout our history and specific areas of life could be re-investigated several times to determine how social values have altered as each generation has made its progression and achieved greater understanding.

Each series of lives is lived by one "physical" soul that is one element of the "total" soul. Between each physical lifetime the "physical" element returns to the "total" soul and a review is made of lessons learned and benefits accrued from each particular lifetime and the next lifetime is adjusted or abandoned according to the next series of investigations to be made, based upon the experience gained in the recently completed life. It is only the "total" soul that is aware of every aspect of itself. Each "physical" soul has lived its lives without an awareness of its twin or triplet or of the "total" soul's existence.

The "Human Plan" has been in place, and operating, for approximately 7,000 years and is approaching its conclusion. As the end has approached, those who have neglected areas of their personal, physical plans have attempted to complete their chosen activities quickly. This has meant a rapid increase in the human population, over the past couple of centuries, as all souls complete their exploration of the human experience. During the twentieth century, a large number of souls have completed their chosen life plans and have begun to amalgamate each separate "physical" soul into one where an increasing level of consciousness can be accommodated.

This amalgamation process should have resulted in an overall reduction in the human population. The reduction has not occurred for two reasons. The first is that there are many members of the six higher civilisations who have chosen to incarnate at this time in order to observe and assist in humanity's transition and have, therefore, replaced the large number of people who are undergoing the amalgamation process. The second reason adds a further level of complexity to the "total" soul's multi-dimensional capabilities.

There are many people who have experience of meditation groups where the group facilitator suggests a "guided" meditation journey. In the travels experienced during this form of exercise some of the most profound occur when the facilitator suggests that those taking part imagine themselves to be animals. Very often, if the species of animal is not specified, the individual will find themselves instantly transported into the body of an animal with which they form an instant, comfortable, rapport.

This instant transition and relaxed acceptance of the experience is because the person is connecting with a part of their "total" soul that is investigating other areas of physical life that are available on Earth. This level of consciousness is very limited as only a very small number of animal species are available for this type of experience. The list of animals is limited by each species' level of consciousness and suitability of energy frequencies. For example, it is possible to live as an eagle but not as a sparrow, a dolphin but not as a shark, a gorilla but not a small monkey. Each animal type allows for new levels of experience and understanding within the total range of physical existences available on the planet.

This aspect of human consciousness is that which gave rise to members of traditional, tribal communities being able to adopt the persona of certain animals. With practice, it is possible to "share" consciousness with the element of an individual's "total" soul that is living as an animal. This does not mean that the person physically changes into the form of the animal, but is able to take on aspects of the animal's sensory systems and behavioural characteristics. In extreme instances, a very few people have been able to alter their own energy fields, or auras, to resemble that of the animal's thereby appearing to "shape shift".

Observers of these very talented people have seen the outline of the animal around the person as the aura shifts frequencies to that of the animal. The person has remained in their original form but their energy fields have undergone total transition. Bears and wolves have been particularly popular choices for the "total" soul's experiences as they have very high levels of sensory awareness. Not all suitable animals are formed by the consciousness given by the "total" soul, but a large minority have been. The majority of animals receive their consciousness from the same source as that of all plants, the planetary consciousness.

As our souls re-combine themselves and our bodies grow in their total consciousness, the aspects that have formed animals is the first element to be withdrawn from its non-human journeyings. Whilst the loss of animals is mainly due to our irresponsible destruction of wildlife habitats, a percentage of the animal population is being lost due to the consciousness re-structuring. It is almost always wild animals that are chosen by the "total"soul as domesticated animals, such as sheep and cows, lack the levels of consciousness awareness required. It should be remembered that in killing these wild animals we have deprived ourselves of an extremely rewarding level of experience.

Animals that are kept as pets, such as cats and dogs, are also not suitable candidates for this type of consciousness experience. This type of animal is connected to the planetary consciousness and is insufficiently aware to be suitable candidates for use by the "total" soul. Much as it is extremely appealing to consider re-incarnating as a domestic cat, it is, unfortunately, not possible. However, their levels of consciousness can, on an individual animal basis, be enhanced by close contact with loving people.

Animals that are kept as pets have a common consciousness that is generated by a kind of mass consciousness applicable to each animal group. For example, a dog mass consciousness or a cat mass consciousness. All animals, of each particular group, are a part of, and connected to, their respective mass consciousness. When individual animals are shown love and respect, by the people with whom they share their lives, they can take on a higher level of individuality. In other words, they become an almost separate consciousness with their own identity and characteristics. When these animals pass out of the physical, they can retain their individuality for some time but, eventually, they will return to their mass consciousness origins.

So it can be seen that all of us are considerably more than we appear to be. There is considerably more to our existence and the soul than most people have assumed. The multidimensional concept is one which many people will have great difficulty in accepting, but it is set to play a much larger role in human affairs than it has throughout all of our history. As each human physical life is completed, the "physical" consciousness returns to the "total" soul and re-combines with it. The accumulated experiences and memories, from all of its many lifetimes, will be "downloaded" into the "total" soul's sum of experience. The percentage consciousness, that comprises each particular "physical" soul, is then available for integration with the "physical" soul that has chosen to remain physical during our transition period. The remaining "physical" soul will slowly begin drawing into itself the remainder of the "total" soul, or consciousness, until it has assimilated all of the consciousness into itself. A complete human being.

The process of re-integration has already begun. As each "portion" of consciousness is drawn back into the "whole human", awareness of the multidimensional self will grow and the past memories, both human and animal, will become part of the "whole human's" memories. These memories will feel as if they are a part of the individual's past, as indeed they are, but they will also be aspects of the self that many will find unusual.

Although each "physical" soul has lived the full range of human experience, they have, generally, adopted one aspect of the human emotional makeup to concentrate upon. Each person is a mixture of kind and cruel, honest and dishonest, reliable and unreliable etc., whatever kind of emotional life the final "physical" soul has lived, in this lifetime, the "whole human" must incorporate all of the other aspects of the emotional spectrum that have been experimented with throughout all of the many lifetimes lived. Some will find it difficult to accept that, although in this lifetime they have lived exemplary lives, they will have memories of, perhaps, acting with extreme cruelty. There will need to be a brief period of adjustment, for each individual, as the reality of these memories is accepted.

There are no competitions within the soul, no sense of winners and losers. As each individual takes on their full consciousness, with all of its conflicting memories, understand that it is these individuals who have best come through their experiences and it is they who have achieved a level of awareness where they are the ones, out of all of the "physical" souls that they represent, who are the most able to cope with full integration.

The period of potential confusion will not last for very long and should be recognised as a period of re-integration of the whole. Each "physical" soul has a story to tell and who better to tell it to than the self. Although this is potentially a period of doubt and confusion, it should be recognised for what it actually is, a time of rejoicing for the period of our suffering is over. This is the long awaited time when we can once again see the reality of our world and the constructive part each of us has played in human history. This is not a time of death, nor is it a time of destruction, but a time of renewal and re-awakenings. It is time for us to live again with the Angels.

Chapter Seven

The Origin of the Soul

The term "soul" has a different meaning and interpretation for each person, ranging in extremes from a feeling of inner suffering that is expressed in a form of music, to those who have experienced the ultimate inner joy felt with the knowing of the connection to the Creator. For many, the "soul" is an abstract concept that is unattainable, for some it is the commonplace aspect of everyday life, whilst for others, it is superstitious nonsense that belongs in the realms of fantasy.

Whatever an individual's views are, the reality is that each and every living thing, throughout this universe, is comprised of a consciousness that has been brought into being by an aspect of the universal consciousness.

The term "soul", in the context of this book, is used as a reference to the higher level of consciousness that brings about elements of Creation that cloak themselves in physical forms, particularly when related to human existence. The Soul is an energy, a level of consciousness, that is a creator in its own right. It generates other forms of life and communicates with the universe and all of its life forms. Each and every consciousness is connected, both in its origins and in its condition of existence. Nothing, in this universe, is outside of the universal soul and communication and interaction between its multitudinous aspects is that which keeps the universe functioning.

Within this universe, the soul, or function of higher consciousness, takes very many forms and shapes that each explores an aspect of existence and evolution. Those aspects of universal consciousness that wish to express their existence as free thinking, free moving and free acting individuals have chosen the form of the humanoid. In other universes, other forms of expression exist which reflect the elements of creation chosen to be explored and experienced. The current sum of Creation amounts to ten different and totally separate universes, each exploring and experiencing a different aspect of potential and possibility.

Within the universe, that our planet is a part of, the aspect of potential being investigated is that of freedom of choice. This freedom of choice extends to all areas of created life and evolution and, ultimately, has no limitations. Each and every individual consciousness has the choice of exploring whatever aspects of Creation that they choose, within this universe.

All consciousness comes from the Creator and the Creator is all consciousness. All of Creation is the sum of all Consciousness. The Creator has created in order to experience all that there is to be experienced by bringing into being separate consciousnesses that are capable of free thought and, therefore, are able to explore all aspects of potential and possibility. Consciousness, in this sense, is that which we call the soul.

The Creator inhabits a realm that is outside of creation and is composed of an energy that allows for limitless possibilities and limitless creation. The Creator itself came about by what could be described as limitless fields of potential combining to form a consciousness. It is these fields of potential that allows the Creator to generate all forms of life. The Creator inhabits the ultimate blank page where all things are possible and all energies exist and where all of Creation begins and ends. Energies of all possible frequencies and wavelengths exist in this space and it is the combining of these energies, in all of their infinite combinations, that provide the potential for the exploration of all possibilities.

Creation commences with the formation of an "envelope" of energy that defines the boundaries of a particular universe. Boundaries are necessary in order to contain the various energies and consciousnesses with which the universe is to be inhabited. Within the confines of this envelope, the Creator instills a consciousness that contains the energy frequencies that are necessary for the aspect of potential that the particular universe is to explore.

In the case of the universe that contains our planet, the universal consciousness is represented by the Thirteen Higher Beings who act as co-creators and "managers" of this universe. The creation of the universal consciousness determines all aspects and forms that all of the inhabitants of that universe will take and is the blueprint for all of that particular creation. The universal energies combine and re-form into their own forms of consciousness and each consciousness finds its own form of expression and level of being. The Thirteen Higher Beings assist each emerging consciousness to choose its own state of existence. This is the primary directive that permeates all levels of existence within this universe, the freedom to choose a level of being.

By using available energies, each consciousness expresses itself in whatever way is compatible with its own abilities and level of awareness. Universal life begins with consciousness patterns that contain massive quantities of energy and, therefore, the highest potential. These energy levels permit the construction of massive structures that allow the other, smaller, forms of consciousness to combine with each other to form galaxies and stars. All forms of life have a consciousness and, therefore, an energy. It is the quantity and frequency of energies, contained within each consciousness, that allows each life form to express its own chosen form and level of existence.

Galaxies, and the stars contained within them, are consciousnesses that have found a level of existence that allows other forms of life to express their own choice of existence and levels of being. This is, perhaps, a difficult concept for most of us to grasp. In the same way as the Creator has consciousness, so has the universe and its galaxies and all levels of life all the way down to animals and plants. Each has a consciousness and a level of existence that is expressed in ways that each consciousness chooses within the constraints of the energy frequencies available.

Each component of this universe is a living, thinking organism that is apart of, and connected to, the universal whole. No living thing exists that is not a part of the structure and purpose of this universes. Our planet is a microcosm of the universal whole, where each living thing interacts and forms an interconnected part of the life on Earth, and so it is with the universe. In order for anything to physically exist, it must first be conscious of the fact that it does exist. It is the conscious awareness of potential that allows all forms of life to exist. In order to exist, life must be consciously aware of its potential.

Throughout our history, we have taken the view that the universe was created for the purpose of creating humanity. This is not the case. Humanity exists because the universal consciousness recognised the potential for physical existence at the level at which we have been evolved. It was the fulfilment of that potential that brought us to life. In the same way as humans have a conscious potential, so do stars and galactic structures. Galaxies exist because the consciousness of each galaxy found a way to express its consciousness in that particular form and structure and it is the level of individual consciousness that makes each galaxy separate. If each galaxy was not a conscious construct, then this universe would only be filled with consciousness with a potential for structure and no life would exist outside of that potential.

All forms of life exist in a shape and structure that is most suited to that form of life. It is the consciousness, or soul, of each life form that provides the structure for that life form to construct its shape around. Astronomers have noted that stars have a life cycle. A star comes into being, lives its life span and then destroys itself. The debris formed by this destruction then re-combines to form itself into a new star. The star was originally formed by a "soul" collecting around itself particular types of energy that bring the new star into being. The completion of its life cycle is brought about by either these energies becoming depleted or the "soul" deciding that it has existed in that particular form for a sufficient length of time and wishes to experience a re-newal of its form in order to gain new experiences.

The consciousnesses that form themselves into galaxies and stars do not all find a suitable form for them to experience their existence but remain in an energy form until such time as the right combination of energies is found. This allows the universal void to be filled and potential to be progressed during the whole life cycle of the universe, producing a spontaneity and re-generation of energies that help prevent the universal energies stagnating. As with all things, the universe itself has a life cycle. The Creator brings it into being and, ultimately, consciousness returns to the Creator.The length of time that each universe exists varies considerably. Consciousness is brought into being and explores and experiences all of its potential until it has reached a point where the energy that generated that potential has been depleted.

The process of return is similar to that of creation but in reverse and involves a time span varying from 200,000 million years to 1,000,000 million years. Each consciousness returns to the Creator at a time of its own choosing. The energies that gave each consciousness, or soul, its form are slowly released and the consciousness re-combines with that of the Creator. The released energies return to their unformed state and either return to the fields of potential of their origin or remain within the universal envelope for further use. The consciousnesses that inhabited the universe, have a choice of remaining as part of the Creator or of commencing a new universal life cycle. The universe that we are a part of is currently mid way through its second life cycle.

As each consciousness re-enters the universal envelope, it collects together the universal energies and combines them into new forms and frequencies and then releases them in an outward rush of creation. The process is like an inward breath followed by a rapid exhalation that fills all of the universal space. It is the memory of this exhalation, or explosion of energies, that has given rise to the concept of the "Big Bang" theory of universal generation and the religious concept of "Spiritus", or Divine Breath.

Once the galactic and star system consciousnesses have settled into their chosen forms of being, other forms of soul expression can then be experienced. Planetary forms are brought into being by either of two processes or a combination of both. The consciousness that has formed into a star, or sun, chooses to use a part of its consciousness to experience life as a separate entity that is capable of generating an atmosphere and creating other forms of life. Alternatively, and most commonly, a new consciousness will take on this role and form itself into one, or more, planetary structures, forming either one planet or a whole solar system.

This is how our solar system came into being. A single consciousness was asked to form thirteen planets with high physical densities that would be capable of generating and supporting forms of life that have an extremely dense physical composition. For a number of reasons, four of these planets were unable to be sustained as individual planets and the part of the solar system consciousness that formed these planets re-combined with the other planets in the solar system, most noticeably with that aspect that is Earth. The energies that had been combined to form these four planets were allowed to dissipate throughout the adjacent galactic structures and have been used to form other worlds. The removal of these four planets had a catastrophic affect on Earth's early history that required rapid and drastic measures to overcome but, eventually, all of the energies were re-combined sufficiently to allow planetary evolution to continue.

Souls that are capable of constructing planetary structures have, as a function of their consciousness, not only the capacity to sustain forms of life but also the ability to generate other forms of life. These simpler life forms are usually represented by planetary flora and fauna. Life forms that have a more human scale need to be created and this is the next stage in the universal generation process. In order to be created, each of the six higher civilisations required a home world, a place where the evolutionary journey could begin.

Some of the earliest planetary structures had generated sufficient atmosphere, together with flora and fauna species, that would make such home worlds places where evolution could commence. The planets were chosen on the basis of their state of preparedness for sustaining life and the planetary consciousness's willingness to help in this early evolutionary stage. The individuals of the six higher civilisations were created as separate consciousnesses that existed at an energy frequency that was compatible with the planet of origin. The only difference between each of the civilisations is this variation in energy frequencies.

Each civilisation began life as a densely compressed consciousness that took on the form of the humanoid. Although their shape is the same as ours, their physical structures are much less dense and, to our eyes, would appear more as a gently defined misty form than physical beings. These beings are composed of a pure energy that requires very little in the way of physical matter. This frequency of energies allowed them to evolve very rapidly into free moving and free thinking beings that also have a very high level of awareness. They are able to communicate directly with all levels of consciousness that exist throughout this universe. Their main point of contact has always been, and continues to be, the Thirteen Higher Beings. However, they are also able to freely communicate with all galactic, star and planetary consciousnesses.

The six higher civilisations form the basis of all of the higher forms of life that followed them in creation. The six rapidly progressed from conscious, but separate, individuals into individuals that function within a mass consciousness that began on a planetary level, but has now evolved to a level where, collectively, they are not far removed from the Thirteen Higher Beings. Each of the six began their evolutionary journey on separate and far distant worlds but now form what could be considered a single combined civilisation, which although maintaining their six separate identities, can also act as a single consciousness.

This act of combining of consciousnesses is the crux of the evolutionary process and is the ultimate goal of this universe's creation. However, the freedom of choice allows each individual to choose whether to combine in this way or not. In the case of the six, their choice was freely and readily made and the benefits to each civilisation, and each individual within each civilisation, are immense. Due to the combined consciousness, the six act as facilitators and co-ordinators for virtually all activity that occurs within the universe. They are able to freely move between stars and planets without the need for any form of "space ship" and do not require any form of atmosphere or "food" to survive. Their method of taking in sustenance is to directly share and combine energies from any energy source available throughout the universe. These sources of energy are the free flowing patterns of energy frequencies that have been made available to facilitate the creation of galaxies, stars and planets. They have, in human terms, an immense life span that can extend up to very many thousands of years. They do not die in the sense that we would describe it, but their consciousness patterns shift into other forms that allow them to either return directly to the Creator or to move on to experience existence as a planetary structure.

With the successful evolution and integration of the six, a further level of existence was created but with a much increased density and a more solid physical form. The evolution and characteristics of the seven minor civilisations have no direct correlation to our existence and, therefore, it is sufficient just to comment that their creation was an evolutionary step on the process of bringing about full physical existence as experienced by human beings.

Planet Earth's solar system was brought into being with the express purpose of generating "physical" life. The term "physical" is a misnoma. Everything that composes the human world is ultimately composed of energy. Objects only appear solid as the energy, of which they are composed, is of a highly compressed nature. Our frequencies of perception are tuned to resonate with these densities allowing the energies to take on the appearance of solid matter. All physical material, including our bodies, is composed of atoms. If these atoms are viewed directly they are seen as particles orbiting around a central core, or nucleus, that generates energy patterns that are powerful enough to maintain these particles in orbit and separate from the nucleus. When viewed in this way, matter is composed of these minute particles, or quanta, that have, proportionately, as much space between them as the planets of the solar system and, as with the solar system, this space is composed of an energy. Even the nucleus and the particles themselves are composed of an energy that takes the form of the vortex. The solidity of the nucleus, proton and electron particles is given by the energy vortices being highly compressed together to such an extent that they appear solid. This is the force that gives nuclear generation and nuclear weapons their immense and virtually limitless power. The explosion generated, in these processes, are the release of the energies contained within these vortices as they rapidly unwind. When viewed in this way, our world ceases to be one of dense, physical matter, but one of immense energy potential.

As soon as our planet was ready, the life generation process began. The planet's atmosphere was ultimately to be composed primarily of oxygen and the early life forms were those which could help bring this atmosphere into being. Life began in two ways, bacteria and other simple organisms were seeded onto the planet by meteorites and comets used as carrier vehicles whilst the planet itself generated simple forms of flora.

When the planet was sufficiently prepared, higher forms of life were introduced. The majority of these forms were designed for life in Earth's oceans and it was in the oceans that most of the early evolutionary paths developed. The formation of so much free water was brought about as it was intended to act as a temperature and atmospheric regulator to help maintain the correct atmospheric balance. The life forms that were seeded onto the planet originated on several other worlds and each was genetically and energetically manipulated for existence at such a high physical density and high oxygenation. Most of these species were an adaption of life forms found on the worlds inhabited by the seven minor civilisations with some others being specially created for the planet. Many forms of life underwent several re-seedings and manipulations until a more purposeful balance was reached allowing for the introduction of life forms capable of accepting individual consciousnesses. Plant and animal life does not possess the capability for totally independent conscious awareness but, instead, share consciousness with the souls around them. Animals and plants are primarily part of the planetary consciousness and form an aspect of what could be called a group soul. Some animals appear to have an individual consciousness but this is brought about by sharing their existence with individual consciousnesses, such as you and me, who express love and respect for these animals.

With the successful colonisation of the planet, other, more advanced, forms were created bearing a suitable humanoid form. These early humanoids did not, as yet, contain a higher consciousness but were a life form that could function within the planetary consciousness at higher levels of awareness. Humans, as we would now be recognised, were not developed until the facilities built on the continent of Atlantis were introduced and genetic engineering techniques could be brought into operation. The genetic engineering methods adopted were very similar to those used by the Creator in creating the life forms that compose the six higher civilisations.

The basic humanoid forms had already been created and found to be functioning well at the planet's electro-magnetic densities. These forms were modified in order for them to have the capability of incorporating individual souls. The raw materials for the human body were supplied by the planet itself, but the soul, the driving force of the material body, came from the individuals of the six higher civilisations. This is who we essentially are and from where we originate. Each of us is an individual from one of the six higher civilisations. DNA and "soul" memory of these origins is that which gives us humans the concept of "Heaven". This is the origin of the human soul and is the place where all humans have, and will, ultimately return. All of human life and experience has been lived as a way of experiencing a new level of being. Throughout the ten universes, that currently compose the sum of Creation, we are unique. No other forms of higher consciousness exist at human levels of existence.

Chapter Eight

The Present

Much has been made of the fact that we are at a point of change. It is all very well to state this as fact but the questions most asked by individuals at the moment are:

What are the changes?

Why are they happening?

What are the implications on an individual level?

What if they do happen?

What if they do not happen?

To start at the beginning.

The Prime Directive was insisted upon by mankind, ourselves, when it became clear, 20,000 years ago, that the planet's electro-magnetic field would have a devastating affect on mankind's higher brain functions. The 20,000 year life cycle was agreed upon to allow us to try to discover, for ourselves, an evolutionary pathway. The six higher civilisations were entrusted with the role of re-awakening us at this current time if we were unable to find our own way back.

Changes are occurring at this point in our history for very many reasons. Some are very simple, some are extremely complex and have far reaching implications throughout the universe. Mankind has free choice in all matters relating to mankind. In order to choose, we must know what our options are. Due to our condensed brain functions and disrupted memory systems, we are not aware of the differences between our current condition and our level of awareness at the time when the planet was first seeded with modern man. If we were fully aware of the differences then it is certain that we would not choose our present condition of sensory deprivation.

The five senses that our children are taught to rely on are but an extremely small part of the sensory systems built into human physiology. Sight, hearing, smell, touch and taste are the sensory equivalents of single notes of music when compared to the symphony of true perception. Throughout the so-called "Developed Countries", we have become so ensnared within our physical environment that anyone displaying signs of sensory perceptions beyond the five physical ones are considered freakish and many individuals, who have become aware of their higher sensory abilities, have suppressed them in order to prevent potential ridicule. Actions such as these are the equivalent of permanently filling the ears with cotton wool and wearing dark glasses.

Consider the difference between the developed countries' view of sensory abilities and those of more naturally orientated peoples. It has been argued that the ability to sense the location of underground water in an arid land or the ability to know what tomorrow's weather will bring is not of much use to a city dweller. But what if the city dweller were able to sense the presence of an assailant around a dark corner or to sense that the car in front is about to swerve to avoid an obstacle or the ability to sense the scent of a flower across a traffic clogged street? Are not these senses of equal value? Scientists are returning to the plant life of the planet for new medicines because synthetic chemical compounds have failed to heal many of our physical illnesses. Would it not be more advantageous if all of us had retained the ability to sense the plant's healing properties just by looking at the plant?

Our current answer to dealing with radioactive nuclear waste is to bury it for 100,000 years in areas where it is hoped there will not be seepage into the ground water or where seismic activity will not occur. Would it not be better if our increased sensory abilities enabled this lethal waste to be neutralised? These examples are some of the potential benefits to ourselves that the current changes have begun to bring. We have the choice of continuing at our present level of evolution or whether we will move onto an evolutionary course that does not stop at the stars.

Before moving on to examine the current changes in more detail, it would be a suitable point to look a little more closely at one major area of the human character that requires some clarification. Lack of understanding has meant that all through history, individuals have allowed themselves to be used by those who would seek power over others. This concept of an individual being of no self worth has become so entrenched in our thinking that any other view is frowned upon.

We need to begin to understand that each person has the right, and more importantly, the ability to be in control of their own lives. None of us are born shackled. Controls and ways of thinking are added as a young child grows. These control systems are all around the child who is gradually de-sensitised to the world around them and manipulated into ways of thinking that stultify growth and potential. Governments, employers, scientific institutions, medical institutions, religious orders, etc. etc. all seek to control by keeping us ill-informed and misinformed to keep populations from thinking for themselves. We should have learned to recognise the symptoms of control, seek for the underlying truth behind events and stop taking the reporting of events at face value.

Individuals must begin to tune into their own feelings and perceptions in order to understand themselves fully and to realise that everyone has a responsibility to themselves, to mankind as a whole and to the planet. This does not mean that paranoia has to take over our perceptions nor does it mean that anarchy should be encouraged. The exact opposite is true. By each individual taking full responsibility for themselves and for their actions, society as a whole benefits and the need for violent actions and reactions diminishes.

Many individuals will find this process of self-discovery an uncomfortable prospect. So many of us build up a false facade around ourselves in order to deal with the manipulations of the world we find around us that after a period of time, the individual begins to believe the false facade and forgets about the real person within. Leave the false facade in place, if the individual feels uncomfortable without it, but learn to re-connect with the feelings and emotions that are trapped within. When the re-connection process has begun, the facade will disappear of its own accord and, like a butterfly emerging from its cocoon, the natural inner beauty of each individual will begin to shine into the world.

Imagine a world where each individual is at peace with themselves and, therefore, at peace with the world around them. Imagine how that would feel and how the world would feel. Imagine a permanent sunny summer's day. Most of us are experiencing an overwhelming feeling for the need for change. The change must start from within. Individual understanding of the self is the key to unlocking our future. Those individuals who are unwilling to undertake the inner journey to re-discovery will miss out on much of our future journey.

Many of us have interpreted this desire for personal change in the form of development of the outer, physical body. It is important to understand that a healthy physical body can only be achieved by exercising and healing the inner self. Diets and rigorous physical exercise only tones the outer shell. If the time and effort expended on physical exercise in recent years had been used instead on the human spirit, mankind would already be treading the higher ground. If every one of us took a couple of minutes every morning to carry out one simple exercise to cleanse and energise the body and spirit, we would already be at peace with ourselves. Find a couple of minutes during the day, preferably in the morning when individuals are relaxed. Stand with the feet together and arms down to the sides, close your eyes and imagine being showered by glowing, bright golden light. Feel the light enter through the top of the head and travel down the spine washing out all of the fears and hurts and toxins and taking them down through the feet and into the ground. It does not matter if you do not live on the ground floor, just imagine that the light travels into the ground.

Next, feel the light continue to come down through the head and leave through the abdomen, as the light shines through the abdomen, feel it wash all over the outside of the body, forming itself into a golden shell all over the body. Leave the shell in place for the rest of the day, checking on it and reinforcing it from time to time. This exercise has two benefits, firstly it cleanses and purifies both the body and the spirit. Secondly, the golden shell helps to protect the individual from harmful thoughts and energies. If you feel self-conscious about carrying out such an odd exercise, do not worry. Find a time when no one else is around and therefore no one else will know. For those who are familiar with such exercises, you will already know of its benefits.

For nearly three hundred years, the other civilisations have been helping to focus new energies onto the planet with one intent: to help to raise our perceptions of ourselves and our planet. In terms of how we measure time, this is a long period, but in terms of a soul's journey, it is but a moment. Individuals have been unable to recall the details of their soul's journeyings and the experience gained. The combined effects of the breaking down of the DNA memory sequences to only two spirals and the splitting of the mind into the conscious and the sub-conscious, has left us with a severely limited view of ourselves and our history. Restoration of these memories can only be achieved by the re-combining of the separated components.

The first re-construction works were commenced in the 1980s. The component parts of the missing eleven strands of the DNA helix have been preserved within the cell structure, floating around as unrecognised debris. These separated components have been slowly re-combining to re-construct the broken strands. As the components have been re-combining, the activity has also been slowly switching on dormant areas of the two helixes, areas that scientists have called junk DNA, and the revised DNA system is gradually switching itself back into action. This is a very delicate process that can only be carried out slowly and with great caution. Re-activating the DNA too quickly could cause our slow neural systems to overload. For this same reason, it will only be possible to re-construct between ten and twelve strands until our physical systems start to catch up. Scientists have noted this change to the DNA structures and have misinterpreted its purpose and have become alarmed by this process. We should not be concerned by this re-construction and any temporary physical side effects are purely transient as the body's systems re-adjust.

The first noticeable effect has been the start of the breakdown of the mind's conscious and sub-conscious veil.

This is most noticeable in children and young teenagers. Many children, particularly at the time of puberty, when the soul fully enters the physical body, will start to have very strong memories of previous lifetimes. The same is true for many adults who, because of accumulated experiences during this current lifetime, will find themselves remembering events that they had long forgotten. Sometimes the resurgence of memories from this lifetime will start to become mingled with re-emerging memories from previous lifetimes. Everyone who is physical on Earth, at this time, is going through this process. Do not be afraid to discuss these memories with others as they will understand, as they are also undergoing a similar experience.

As with all transitionary periods, some discomfort might arise. Recognise them for what they are: symptoms of a recovery and any discomfort will pass very shortly. Everyone who is physical at this time has volunteered to be a part of this evolutionary process. Each and every human is physical for this purpose and each and every one of us has a role to play. We must fully understand the importance of our presence at this time and that nothing will be attempted that each one of us, on an individual basis, is not capable of dealing with. Many individuals are equipped to make a smooth transition during this initial phase and are, therefore, able to assist those who experience difficulties. If you are a parent, listen to what your children have to say. The children are literally mankind's future. Listen to what they have to say and treat their comments with understanding and respect. Try to work against the conditioning that you have been subject to and allow these new ideas and concepts to gently push the old ways of thinking away.

Every single one of us has had many past lifetimes. Some will remember lifetimes on other worlds and as a part of other civilisations. Try not to fight against or deny these memories as they arise, they are a part of each individual, a part of your heritage and the beginnings of a new understanding. Many have come to the planet to share in the work of awakening and are experiencing a physical lifetime for the first time. The memories held by these individuals will not include previous lifetimes on Earth, but of other worlds, which at first might feel very strange. Do not be confused by these memories. There are many individuals who are in this position and you are therefore not alone.

The planet is now receiving energies that have not been available to us for many centuries. As the planet and all of its forms of life start to assimilate these energies, some physical effects will become apparent. Some of these affects will be very subtle and hardly noticeable. Others will be very strong and of a global scale. The planet is a living entity and has already undergone several changes that are a direct response to the changes of energy frequencies. The planet has always "wobbled" about on its polar axis. Scientists are aware of the wobble and monitor its rate of change. The recent axial shift was stronger than was predicted, 4% instead of 2%, but the shift is not strong enough to cause any physical damage and, certainly, the planet is not set to wobble itself to pieces as has been predicted by some. Earth's land masses have also always been subject to movement as the planet's own energy systems re-adjust themselves to our careless activities. Whilst there has been an increase in the magnitude of seismic activity, there has not been any increase in the magnitude of seismic movements. Some continents might, however, experience seismic movements where there have been none in the past, but these will be temporary and will not be very destructive.

Much of the planet's plant life will also benefit from new energies that will promote increased growth and more abundant flowering blooms. Many areas of derelict land will now produce new growths as natural plant species increase in strength. Naturally occurring plants that are used for food and medicines will increase their potency and flavour. However, it should be noted that a number of plants that have been genetically altered will not be strong enough to take on these energies and a number of crops will progressively fail. Animals will also undergo change. Most species will become strengthened and an increasing number of species, that were once thought extinct, will be re-discovered. It is also true, however, that several species, that have been weakened to the point of extinction by our unthinking attitudes and actions, will cease to exist at all.

Many of us will also experience physical symptoms of change. These physical symptoms are as a direct result of our DNA structures re-combining and re-adjusting. All symptoms caused by this process are temporary and are more likely to cause the reduction of diseases and infections than to cause the end of a physical life. These are some of the likely symptoms: an increase in mild viral strains, many of which have not been previously noted by doctors; short periods of feeling light headed and dizzy; possible slight movements of the spinal column as the body's physical channels for the energy system become energised.

There will be other symptoms that will be experienced on an individual basis, but the three listed above are likely to be the most common. Our emotional systems will also respond to the new energy flow. As with memories, deep seated emotions, that have not been allowed to be expressed, will now surface and must be dealt with responsibly and fully in order to release the physical tensions and restrictions that constraints on the emotions can cause. There are, of course, other benefits. This period of change is also a period of great healing. Some of those who have suffered long term illnesses or physical injury will recover. Whilst others who received physical injuries, will begin to understand that their injuries have been for a purpose and will, therefore, be able to come to terms with the disruption to their lives. As with individuals, deep seated, unresolved memories and emotions, will rise to the surface on social, genetic and, perhaps, national levels. This does not mean that there will be conflict on a global level. The Gulf war, former Yugoslavia and several African countries have seen conflicts arise as the emotional memories have become unlocked. Other conflicts have arisen as groups of individuals have attempted to remove the influence of an oppressive regime.

Attempts have been made, by the other civilisations, to try to prevent armed conflict arising, but their influence can only extend so far in such situations. It has been within, and continues to be within, the power of national and world organisations and governments to have prevented these armed conflicts arising. As has been the case throughout human history, it is only when economic advantages are threatened, as in the Gulf war, that peace keeping actions have been given sufficient impetus to be effective. It has always been an aspect of human nature that certain individuals will attempt to seize control of one section of a population by inflaming the emotions of another. There will be instances when such individuals will attempt to take advantage of this brief period of emotional resurgence. Wherever and whenever this situation arises, we must direct thoughts of peace towards these areas and peace keeping forces must be allowed to act effectively if armed conflict breaks out.

It is time for mankind to seize the initiative for peace on a global level. It is appreciated that at a time when individual emotions are operating at a highly active level that it will be difficult for individuals not to resort to acts of violence, but it must be understood that the emotional turmoil is part of the process of progressive healing and, therefore, the energies generated by these emotions should be released in as peaceful a way as possible.

Those of the other civilisations, that are working with mankind, are making every effort to ensure that peace is maintained. However, the impetus for peace and change can only come about if each individual wishes it to be so. Without mankind's assent the other civilisations cannot act.

As these changes progress on an individual level, many aspects of human life will fall under close scrutiny and, due to enhanced perceptual abilities, areas of adverse activity that have been tolerated or ignored will become increasingly unacceptable to the individual. Actions taken by individuals, or groups of individuals, to right these wrongs, should be very carefully considered: will the actions taken to right these wrongs prove to be more harmful than the original wrong? Consider all options before taking action. More harm than good could be done and that would be worse than taking no action at all.

Governments also have a responsibility to adopt a flexible approach to these changes, although it is more difficult for a government to respond quickly to changes than it is for an individual. But change they must. The old order that gave governments their authority and power is rapidly breaking down and all governments, the world over, increasingly do not reflect public needs and concerns. It does not matter what shade of the political spectrum each individual government represents, if they no longer act in accordance with their people's wishes they will lose all authority. The lesson of Northern Ireland should be learned and learned well. Peace did not come about because the politicians made it happen. The people of Northern Ireland, and those in other parts of the world who lent them their support, were the ones who brought about peace by their collective will acting on the collective consciousness. Each individual willing the peace to happen, made it happen. Whilst the politicians are still bickering about the details, the people have their victory.

Although there is still the occasional senseless act, the mood for violence has gone and the peace will prevail. This is how each individual can make a real difference: by consciously willing a positive change, the change can occur. Do not wait for someone else to start the process.

When we entered into the great experiment of physical existence, twenty thousand years ago, it was known that at the start of the twentieth century the opportunity for change and re-balance would occur. The arm of the great spiral galaxy that contains the planet's solar system has made its great sweep across the universe into areas where abundant and renewing energies exist in vast quantities. The other civilisations, who were charged with the task by mankind, have helped direct these energies to where they have been needed most and are providing help to those who ask for assistance. Mankind is not only capable of regaining all that it lost all of those centuries ago, but also of moving into a potential future that has no precedent in the history of the universe.

It is now not possible for us to prevent the slow death of our planet by ourselves. Unless we grasp this opportunity wholeheartedly and joyfully, the wonders of Earth will be lost. We have acted unknowingly in ways that have caused mortal damage. The planet will not be allowed to die fully, but we would not be a part of its future. This would be a tragedy of unlimited potential. Much time has been wasted during the years of this century whilst mankind fought for this chance of change and time is now short.

The work of re-construction must start whilst the new energies are abundant and fresh. If we hesitate for too long, the opportunity will be lost and the consequences of that are dire. If only we all knew how much those who are here to help desperately wish to be allowed to help. Each individual holds the key that unlocks the door that allows in the refreshing winds of change. The first step is to want the changes to happen.

An attempt has been made in this chapter to try to show what our options are. The choice of actions lie with us. There are no judgmental forces waiting to pounce if we truly wish to stay as we are, but there are those who, with love and understanding, are ready to help mankind through the temporary difficulties of transition.

The other civilisations have agreed to help mankind for two reasons. The first is that mankind is a part of the other civilisations and has undertaken a task, that of evolution in a physical form, that has benefited the other civilisations in providing knowledge that could not have been learned in any other way and, at the request of mankind, this particular period of time is the most suitable for the conclusion of what could be called the human experiment. Secondly, the energies involved in assisting the work of mankind has meant that other potential areas of development have been delayed. If we are able to take our rightful place within the universe, the energies freed, and the knowledge gained, will prove to be of immeasurable importance.

If an individual wishes to take an active role in their own and mankind's transition, it is very simple. Find a quiet time in your day and sit comfortably, close your eyes and slowly clear your mind. When you are relaxed, just say to yourself: I am here to assist in mankind's progression, I wish to be a part of that progression. Your thoughts will be heard. For those who attend a church, add this thought to your prayers and your prayers will be heard. The wish or prayer must be sincere. If the individual is only looking for personal gain from this situation, they will not be helped. Each individual must look into themselves and know who they are. If the motivation is sincerely for individual expansion, they will quickly feel the energies for change come close to them and they will begin the process of leaving their cocoon. It will be a temptation, by some individuals, to think to themselves, that if the world is changing in any way, and the changes will be of personal benefit, whether I do something or not, then I do not need to do anything but sit back and wait. This free ride will not occur. Those individuals who sincerely wish to assist in the transition will be helped, individually, to make their personal transition successful. Those who choose not to take an active role in the transition process, will stay as they are and will be allowed to continue their existence at their present level of understanding. The process of transition is for our benefit and cannot progress if we do not wish it to. Each individual has the right to choose their part, or otherwise, that they have to play in this work.

Chapter Nine

Current and Future Possibilities

All things are possible.

This is not an empty statement but a statement of fact, the fulfilment of a promise made twenty thousand years ago. We have the potential to make a leap in existence that is unprecedented in the history of the universe. Whether this monumental shift occurs or not is entirely in our hands. All of the pieces are now in place for us to remove the chains that have bound us in our physical ignorance and held us in a spiral of downward destruction.

The energies for change have been subtly raining down on Earth since the beginning of the twentieth century. Their time for potential renewal is rapidly waning and our opportunity for change will not last very long beyond the first decade of the rapidly approaching millenium. If we are to fulfil our true potential, then acceptance of change must begin now. We have been sidetracked too many times during this century, and several opportunities have already been lost. There is a great deal of sympathy, amongst those who are here to assist, for our predicament and the apparent lateness of the hour. There appears to be a vast amount of work still to be done as many of us are still consciously unaware of the possibilities that await us. However, all it takes is for the majority of people to consciously will the change to occur and it can happen within three months. This is the power of the energies and the actual state of readiness of humanity.

Change can only occur if the will for change exists and choices can only be made on the basis of the information available. Information can spread only by open discussion of ideas and concepts. If there is no discussion then there are no new ideas and instead of forward movement into new areas of growth, old ideas are re-cycled and stagnation occurs. The reason for this book is to stimulate discussion and break down the stagnation cycle, to provide a framework for new areas of thought and to answer some of our fundamental and far reaching questions. It has also been intended to show how our thinking and understanding have been progressively narrowed into rigid areas of part truths and false interpretations until the Earth has been seen as being dominated by purely physical parameters. The irony is that we are not even physical but, in our true form, we are a glowing energy that sparkles and shines with a vitality and brightness that can be a beacon of hope for other worlds.

Every person, that has been born, since the end of the last century, have been on the planet for one purpose. This purpose is to aid, and to be a part of, our transition. As the century turned, and the new energies began to be received, a new awareness and seeking after truths has been apparent all over the planet. New areas of information and forms of communication began to open up and mankind began to see itself as something more than just a physical organism. Several writings were produced that began to investigate mankind's true history and many began to remember their past lives and past successes. Most of those who were the vanguard of this new awakening had lived lifetimes directly related to the Egyptian civilisation and it was this civilisation that formed the basis of much of the early beginnings of greater understanding.

This part of our history was chosen as it was the first of our civilisations that had been discovered and was beginning to be understood by scientists and archaeologists in ways which reinforced the emerging memories and channelled writings that were also beginning to appear. At the same time, all of mankind was feeling a need to break away from past experiences and move into a new future. Despite the First World War, and in a way, because of the First World War, the world did change and people's perceptions of themselves and the social structures changed to a degree where everything of the past was left behind. The people of that time recognised their power to change and found the courage to make the change happen. This same recognition, of individual and collective power, needs to be found within those currently alive and the same level of courage needs to be brought with it.

This is not the courage needed to face an adversary, nor is it the courage to take on the world, but it is the courage needed to look into the self and recognise the potential within. It is a quiet courage and a courage that says I can be me and I can fulfil my chosen task. This is all that is required. No fireworks, no giant banners, just the quiet inward journey to the self, where all answers will be found. This is not a journey into selfishness, but a journey to understanding and remembering, a journey of learning what each and every individual has to give to the world and no gift, when given with love, is too small. For each individual has brought into this life a gift. A gift so precious that no one may take it from you, but one which is yours to give. This gift is the self. All of the light and joy that each person will find hidden away within themselves is theirs to give. No outward, physical generosity will do. Money and goods have no value in this exchange. Those with only money and power have the least to give and the most to gain from their inner journeyings. Real wealth can only be measured in terms of spirit and love. No other currency ever existed.

"The Changes" are really a return of past abilities and a conquering of the planet's electro-magnetic fields. There is no magic in this, just a grasping of available opportunities. The main method of acknowledging a person's willingness to fulfil their role has been outlined in a previous chapter of this book. If the commitment is sincerely made, then the life and energies of that person will change. The first step is that the "spirit guides" who work most closely with that person, will make themselves known. This will not usually be a direct approach, such as a ghost-like visit, but their presence will be shown in subtle ways such as objects disappearing or a visit during a meditation.

It should be remembered that one of the frequencies of love is joy and from this joy comes a well developed sense of humour. When people begin to acknowledge, and work with, their "guides", the humour will be noticed and the great humour and joy that normally accompanies this close association will be allowed to grow. As the individual re-energises their connections with their own higher consciousness, the energies lift to a new high. The world, and their view of it, becomes re-newed and the connectedness of all things becomes increasingly apparent. Everyday worries and fears lose their significance and the world appears a brighter place. The underlying reasons behind our activities become clear and begins to be seen for what they are, an obscure veneer hiding the true purposes and joys of life. It is suddenly as if a fog lifts and the clarity of view is startling in its brilliance. The senses take on a new level of awareness. Colours brighten and strengthen in hue. Sounds seem to develop new depths and harmonics that give music a greater meaning. The scent of flowers lifts the spirit higher than was thought possible with their subtlety and depth of fragrance. The taste of food is enhanced with flavours and textures have a new vibrancy to the touch.

Other, long forgotten, senses begin to emerge. The auras around people, animals and plants become increasingly obvious. The shining, inner glow of other people becomes apparent and a feeling of belonging and sharing the planet and all of its forms of life starts to be felt. Life takes on a feeling of vibrancy and a humour that cannot be described in words but can only be felt at an inner, higher, level. This is just the beginning.

When the individual begins to welcome in the new energies for change and starts to properly connect, the higher senses begin to develop. The veil between the conscious and sub-conscious mind begins to lift and understanding of the individual's many levels of existence begins to be felt. The body becomes lighter and freer, old aches and ailments disappear, never to return. The knowledge for self-healing is remembered and dis-ease becomes a forgotten aspect of life. Communication with the "spirit guides" becomes easier and awareness and communication with "Angels" is possible (Angels are generally members of the six higher civilisations in disguise - watch out for the occasional fancy dress outfit). The ability to talk to others on a psychic level begins. An awareness of the mass consciousness develops as does the ability to work inside it. This allows the individual to help modify negative thoughts and moods throughout all of humanity. Beyond these levels, there are no limits and we do not have a vocabulary that includes the words to describe any of the ascending stages with sufficient clarity and superlatives.

This description is just a taster, something that says here is the start. Many have begun this road and many more are about to take the first steps. This road is open to everyone. Nobody needs to be excluded from the pathway of life and the stars and the road begins at your own front door.

Many will no doubt be saying, that they are not worthy of such joys and wonders, that somehow, they are less than others. Each person, as an individual, is ruled by their thoughts. It is who the person thinks they are that makes them fit their thoughts. This is why the start of the process, the inner journey, is so important. When an individual breaks out of their negative thoughts and begins to see the bright spark of being that is within, then negativity is banished. The light of being fills all dark spaces once it is allowed to glow. Nobody, not one single person, is less than another. All have their own gift to give.

To many of us, the last years of the twentieth century, have a dark tinge that is filled with violence and deprivation and question how, if there are such vibrant, re-newing energies at work on the planet, can such deprivations exist. The answer to this question is, on one level, very complex, whilst on another, it is very simple. Every person has lived many lifetimes in the process of karmic re-generation. The re-cycling has allowed individuals to re-balance all imbalances generated throughout all of these successive lifetimes. Each life has been planned to allow the individual the opportunity to undo injustices and right wrongs that occurred in the process.

Each incarnation brought new opportunities and new challenges. The freedom to choose a course of action has been absolute. With this freedom of choice comes the possibility to advance, by resolving these imbalances, or to "carry forward" the hard work to the next lifetime. Many people have taken the easy option, enjoy this life and the difficult work can be resolved the next time around, forgetting that there was a finite amount of time available. With the start of the twentieth century, and the realisation that their last opportunity was upon them, many people have attempted to cram several lifetimes worth of work into one. This has, understandably, produced a confused and a confusing situation. Remember, in human life, there is no such thing as coincidence. Every action has a purpose, it is the reaction, the way in which a situation is dealt with, that causes the problems.

Each and every action, whether an act of kindness or an act of apparent violence, is made with love. This might not appear to be the case, particularly in the case of a violent act. We have become used to thinking in physical terms and have forgotten the existence of the higher realms of consciousness. In any act of violence, there is a perpetrator and a "victim". It is the victim, as part of their pre-life plan, who has asked for the violence to occur as part of their growth and learning process. The attacker is the one who has agreed to share in that particular event. It might appear very strange that someone wants to be a victim but, in some instances, this has been a path to growth and greater understanding, but mainly it is to balance a similar act of violence where the current "victim" was the then perpetrator.

Everything balances in the end. Human life cannot be viewed as purely occurring in one specific physical life span. A human lifetime is measured from the time of arrival, on the planet, until the time of departure from the planet, however many thousands of years and hundreds of lifetimes that entails.

The eye for an eye principle can only work if successive lifetimes allow sufficient time for each individual to re-balance the wrongs. Therefore, although our societies appear to be disintegrating, because of what are, apparently, an increasing number of seemingly senseless acts of violence, it is not the case. Each situation arises because both the victim and the aggressor have agreed that it should occur. If we can understand this concept, then all acts of violence can be viewed from the correct perspective. Nobody is the victim, violence will only occur when it is intended to occur and the fear of random violence is totally unnecessary. If it is part of a person's life plan for an act of violence to occur, at some time during that life, then it will have probably occurred by now. If an act of violence is not part of a person's life plan, there is no reason to assume that such an act will occur. There is no need to fear. The energy generated by fear can literally cripple all other mental functions and the person, that is afraid, cannot live their lives to the full. Nothing major happens, in a person's life, that they have not planned to be there. The triumphs and failures occur at the right times in an individuals life. Periods of depression and despair only occur if that person has forgotten that the situation they are in, is related to an opportunity for growth and expansion. Each and every incident can, and should, be viewed in this way and no matter how bad a situation appears, on the surface to be, the underlying purpose is for growth and re-balance.

Other, seemingly random, acts of personal destruction are also occurring at this time. Drug abuse has been a growing problem that has serious implications. Children, in particular, are extremely vulnerable, at this time, to the potential harm that drugs can engender. Over the past few years, most of the children that have been born are on the planet for the purpose of bringing the potential for change to fruition. These children have arrived with a clean page of life with no, or very little, karmic re-balancing work to complete. As these children have reached puberty, and therefore full consciousness, they have woken to the fact that the world is not as they anticipated. Teenagers, throughout history, have always been disillusioned with the world and have attempted to change it. The current generation expected to be in a changed world. Most of the old orders, and certainly the old ways of thinking, are still, largely, in place.

As these children have grown, the old forms of brain washing and tunnel vision have gradually been imposed upon them.

When they have reached their full consciousness, this has conflicted sharply with their sub-conscious expectations. This has led to such a severe conflict, that in certain individuals, the only way that they can deal with the situation is to shut down their minds and consciousnesses with mind altering drugs. This is obviously not the case with all teenagers, but for many, this is the underlying cause of their problems. Many of the children, that have been born in the last ten years, have arrived with a greater knowledge and awareness of the world than their parents. As they have grown, most have made an adjustment to their expectations, but for many, the shock of realisation has been too great. Those who have made the adjustment have been patiently biding their time until we were all ready to change. When the change begins, in earnest, these children will be ready to lead the world into its long awaited future. Do not deny these children as they are the future of mankind. All parents should open their minds and listen to the message that these children bring with them. The process of education never stops, all people continue to learn as they grow older. Perhaps it is now time to learn from those who are younger and have the light of the stars in their eyes.

As the end of the twentieth century approaches, all of us are completing our cycles of karmic re-balancing. All of the trials and tribulations that have beset people's lives are starting to cease. As these cycles of turmoil and strife are being completed, a new awareness is beginning to unfold. The final release of the energies, tied up in the re-balancing process, can now be turned to positive development. A door is closing on the past and people are emerging from the gloom into a new light. It is as if a page, in each person's personal history has been turned, and they stand on a blank page of possibility. Past events have served their purpose and history is being consigned to the furthest reaches of memory. Our minds are beginning to clear and the chains that tied an individual to their past are being broken. As each act of re-balancing is completed, the individual begins to feel free and re-born.

The time has arrived to forget previously accepted patterns of thought and the old ways of understanding. It is time to forge mankind's new future and each individual has a part to play.

There are a few who have, unfortunately, not taken advantage of opportunity as it has arisen, and for them, a new future is also possible, but not as part of the main progression. This does not mean that they are to be abandoned to some hell nor will they be judged, but they will be treated with love and understanding and helped to regain their place in the universe.

The human mass consciousness has begun to change. The need for peace and the end of all conflict pervades many levels of our awareness. There is a slow recognition of the ending of the re-balancing process and there is a calming of the usual buzz of frantic activity.

Not all work is yet complete and there are some areas of our lives that still require a major overhaul. Some countries have yet to really begin the process of self-realisation, and for them, the near future will prove to be one of rapid change. But these realisations and activities, although sometimes painful, will not last for very long and the whole planet will be in a position to turn to a new blank page of human history.

We have become accustomed to conflict. There has always been one more mountain to climb. As each individual completes their personal re-balancing process, the mountains disappear and the flat plateau comes into view. To many, that are reaching this point, the view is a little unnerving. If there is no more conflict how can there be life? This is the usual question from those who arrive. We constantly wish for a calm, peaceful life, and yet, once we find it, we panic and claim to be bored. The plateau is deceptive, it allows a breathing space of calm, but it also is the start of a stairway. No more slippery slopes, but a gentle, measured upward path that leads as high as each person will let it. There is only one way to cross the plateau - put one foot in front of the other.

A selection from over 100 other titles published by Capall Bann.
A free detailed catalogue is available on request.

The Healing Book **by Chris Thomas & Diane Baker**

This book is for those who wish to heal. The book starts at the beginning of the healing process with simple, easily followed exercises which can begin to unlock the healing potential which is inherent in all of us. Nobody needs to feel left out of these abilities. Whatever level of experience you have of healing, this book explains in simple uncomplicated language that does not use mysticism or any form of ritual. These methods apply equally to humans and to animals. If you do not have any experience of giving healing, but would like to learn, this book can set you on that path. If you already work as a healer, in whatever capacity, and would like to explore your greater potential, this book is also for you.

ISBN 186163 053 0 £8.95

Working With The Merlin - Healing People and Planet **by Geoff Hughes**

The Merlin is a guardian of this planet, together with many others and is acting on behalf of other unseen guardians, seeking mankind's help in restoring harmony to all here. This book is about the Merlin and his teachings in the 1980's and 1990's. The Merlin has awoken, for now is his time to move about the Land again to bring healing to the peoples, the lands and the earth. The writer is, like many others, on a Quest. The Quest for knowledge, to Know, to search for a meaning of life and what things are all about. The answers which came through are stunning, sometimes shocking, often controversial. This book is about aspects of this work, carefully graded to take the aspiring student through the first principles and onward into the realms of having the ability to make direct contact with the Forces of the Cosmos. Cutting through the mountains of superstition and man-made rules to find the simplicity and purity of our natural heritage of direct contact with the Unseen Worlds.

ISBN 186163 0018 £10.95

Practical Meditation **by Steve Hounsome**

A truly practical book which assists us to learn to use meditation in our daily lives, to help reduce tension and promote better reactions in mind and body. "Practical Meditation" separates meditation techniques into easily defined areas, such as breathing exercises, relaxation techniques and healing meditations and there is a full section on learning to "ground" oneself so that the reader can keep their feet firmly on the ground and functioning to their best in the everyday world. The book aims to take the mystery out of meditation, making this ancient practice available to an ever widening group of people. The meditations are explained in terms which are easy to understand and are written for people from all walks of life who are showing an increased interest in meditation.

ISBN 1898307 58X £10.95

Self Enlightenment **by Mayan O'Brien**

Are you on a quest for truth, knowledge and wisdom? If so, this book will be a guide and a stepping stone for you. *Self Enlightenment* is full of practical advice on many areas of life. It discusses meditation, visualisation, the aura, examining our lives, creating a mind map, using astrology, the University of the solar System (a guided visualisation), the Tree of Life, health and herbs and how to organise a retreat for yourself. This book can be seen as a beacon to illuminate your way.

ISBN 186163 0484 £9.95